The Essential Houdini

William Pack

The Essential Houdini

Copyright © 2010 by William Pack

www.williampack.com

Printed in USA

For all those historians before me that
found new treasures in old history.

I truly stand on the
shoulders of giants.

Table of Contents

Acknowledgements

FIRST, IT is important to realize that the information in this book is drawn mostly from secondary sources. It is the distillation of the research of Harold Kellock, William Gresham, Milbourne Christopher, Kenneth Silverman, William Kalush and Larry Sloman. All of those authors did research with primary sources and all wrote fine biographies about Houdini. You should seek out at least one to read.

I need to thank Kay Rogers Henderson, Don Lindman, and Frank Rutledge for being my initial readers and editors. Elaine Cassell, as always, provided the final changes and valuable suggestions. Their great advice and patient corrections made this book possible. Any mistakes in this manuscript are exclusively the fault of the stubborn author.

All images are from the author's collection unless otherwise noted.

Houdini's favorite portrait
(Library of Congress)

Introduction

HOUDINI HAD been dead for fifty-three years when we met. I became acquainted with him at the Back of the Yards Library on the southwest side of Chicago, 47th Street. He lived in the pages of a book, *The Great Houdini* by Beryl Williams and Samuel Epstein. My nine-year-old self hung on every word. His brushes with death and narrow escapes had all the derring-do of one of those old-time movie serials. Best of all, it was true.

I imagined myself with supernatural powers that allowed me to laugh at danger and look suave in a tuxedo. I wanted to be Houdini, just like my friends wanted to be Superman, James Bond, or a World Series winning pitcher for the Chicago Cubs...except Houdini actually existed.

While those friends became computer programmers, accountants, and salesmen, I became a magician. I've performed magic shows for over thirty years. I've spoken on and written about the history of magic in Chicago during the Victorian era.

And ever since I met him, Houdini's legend has

3

fascinated me. I'm not the only one. Decades after his death Houdini still fascinates both young and old. An Amazon.com search shows that there are over 1,000 books related to Houdini, with new ones being written every year. His name is used to sell such diverse products as golf clubs, bottle openers, and computer software. Yet, what do you really know about Houdini?

For thirteen years, I managed a magic store at Chicago's #1 tourist attraction, Navy Pier. Hardly a day would go by without someone asking me about Houdini. That is when I learned that most of what people thought they knew about Houdini was wrong.

The legends have grown so great that one woman actually asked me if Houdini was a real person. She thought he was a fictional character.

In writing this book, I hope to correct some of the misconceptions about Houdini's life.

The problem, though, is Houdini. He made up many of those stories. Ever since he changed his name from Ehrich Weiss to Harry Houdini, he began creating the myth that is HOUDINI. Some of his early biographers helped along by adding their own details to the stories. Subsequent movies and plays written about him may have been long on entertainment, but they were short on history.

The thing is, when you read the real story you realize...the truth is better.

By no means do I presume to have a monopoly on the truth. Everything you read here is the distillation of the consensus view from the main Houdini biographies. Even the best-researched books, *Houdini* by Kenneth Silverman and *The Secret Life of Houdini* by William Kalush and Larry Sloman, disagree on some points. Nor is this meant to be a comprehensive biography; it is only the essentials. I hope after reading this that you will seek out one of the other books for the complete story. There is so much more to tell.

His story is uniquely American. It is an immigrant story, full of struggle and success, danger and drama, humor and heartbreak. He lived at the turn of the century and became a symbol of this new time when anything was possible. His story is a motivational one; in shedding the shackles that bound him, both literally and figuratively, he inspired generations to dream that they could do the same.

He was more than an escape artist. He was a magician, showman, master publicist, historian, collector, writer, inventor, teacher, aviator, philanthropist, scientist, moral crusader, athlete, loving husband, and devoted son.

He was the highest paid performer of his time and the most famous man in the world.

He was a superman, but had all the personal complications of the every man.

He was The Great Houdini.

Houdini the messenger boy (Library of Congress)

Chapter One
America

THE MOVE meant risk, hardship. It meant separation, not knowing when he would again see his wife and five sons. It also meant a chance at a better life. So Mayer Samuel Weisz left his family in the recently combined towns of Buda-Pest in 1876 and sailed to America.

When he married Cecilia Steiner in 1863, he was a widower with a young son, Armin (b.1862) and twenty years older than his new bride. He listed his profession as a soap-maker. Yet, years later there would be unsubstantiated stories of him going to law school, becoming a solicitor, and teaching at a university, perhaps initiating the future Houdini in a family tradition of twisting truth into legend.

There is also no record of his schooling as a rabbi, yet he found a job in Appleton, Wisconsin as just that. There, a small Jewish community of 75 worshipers, with no synagogue, met in a donated room above a saloon. On only a meager salary, Rabbi Weisz saved for two years and finally brought his family to America.

They arrived in July of 1878 with the influx of many immigrants and like those same immigrants; they immediately learned America meant challenge and change. The first barrier was language. They spoke only German, Hungarian, and Yiddish.

A German translator probably filled out their immigration papers, which accounts for the German-English changes in their names. Weisz became Weiss. Armin became Herman, Nátàn Josef (b.1870) became Nathan Joseph, Gottfried Vilmos (b.1872) became William Gottfried, Erik (b.1874) became Ehrich, and Ferencz Deszö (b.1876) became Theodore Franz. Due to a translation error from the Jewish calendar to the Gregorian calendar, the birthday of Ehrich changed from March 24 to April 6. He chose to celebrate it that way for the rest of his life.

In the autumn of 1879, Cecilia gave birth to a sixth son, Leopold David. The family was poor, but surviving. The oldest boys helped contribute as they could. The youngest boys went to school, if only intermittently.

Appleton was an idyllic child's playground, full of picnicking parks and surrounded by woodlands. Livestock still roamed the streets. Never one to shy away from adventure, young Ehrich took advantage of it all.

He also began to show remarkable talents as an athlete and a love of the show. Not having the price of a ticket, he snuck in to see his first circus and discovered his first hero, a tightrope walker. Ever resourceful, Ehrich scrounged up enough rope, tied it as tightly as he could between two trees and, despite many bone-jarring falls, suffered the rope until he walked it.

One other by-product of the circus coming to town was what Houdini called his "professional debut." During October, Ehrich's friend Jack got it into his head to stage a backyard circus. In Houdini's telling, he was the star performer of Jack Hoeffler's 5¢ Circus.

"Ehrich, The Prince of the Air," performed in his red long johns, the pretend tights of a circus acrobat. He said he performed tricks on the trapeze including hanging upside down and picking pins off the ground with his eyelids. In an earlier version of his story, he picked up those pins with his teeth. This was just some of Houdini's life-long practice of myth building. In reality, the tricks were probably average, beginner stunts. However, Houdini needed everyone to believe in his greatness.

Those joys of Appleton would be short lived. By 1883, just as the years of Rabbi Weiss' hard work was to pay off with the building of a synagogue, he was dismissed. He was too old and too old world for his congregation. They wanted someone younger, modern. Someone who would speak the services in English.

As brilliant and cultured a man as Samuel Weiss may have been, English would always elude him. This seems to be more stubbornness (later manifest both positively and negatively in Houdini) than anything, and it would also make it impossible for him to earn any sort of real living.

Years later Houdini spoke about this downturn in their lives "One morning my father awoke to find himself thrown upon the world, his long locks of hair having silvered in service, with seven children to feed, without a position, and without any visible means of support. We thereon moved to Milwaukee, Wisconsin, where such hardships and hunger became our lot that the less said on the subject the better."

Houdini did more than refuse to talk about the hardships in Milwaukee; he practically erased the time there from his history. There were a few bright spots, but in Houdini's telling, they happened in Appleton, not Milwaukee.

The family lived as nomads, moving over four times in the first year, always one-step ahead of the rent collector. Their financial situation was dire.

Rabbi Weiss could not find regular work. His sons helped by working odd jobs. Nine-year-old Ehrich worked as a shoeshine and as a newsboy for the *Milwaukee Journal*. It helped little.

If things in Milwaukee weren't difficult enough, Samuel's oldest son, Herman, added emotional stress. In 1884, Herman moved out of the house, changed his last name to Wise, and married outside the religion.

That was just the start. Herman got sick and moved to

New York, which he hoped would improve his health. By November, he was in the hospital, and on December 24, 1885, he died of tuberculosis. He was twenty-two years old.

Samuel Weiss was overcome with grief. He took to bed and gathering his children around him, asked them to swear an oath to take care of their mother if anything happened to him. In Houdini's recollection of this event, he changed the date of the oath to his father's deathbed and deleted his other brothers out of the scene, his father making the plea to him alone.

Dramatics aside, his father eventually recovered.

At twelve years old, Ehrich decided to lessen the burden on the family and ran away. We know little about his time on the road. He made his way southwest and ended up in Delavan, Wisconsin. A Mr. and Mrs. Flitcroft took him in, sheltered him, and fed him as he looked for work. The adult Houdini never forgot their kindness. He sent them splendid gifts, often salted with generous sums of money, until their deaths.

Work was scarce. He hoofed twenty-five miles to bigger towns like Beloit in his search. From Hannibal, Missouri, he sent a postcard to his mother:

"Dear Ma, I am going to Galvaston Texas and will be home in about a ~~jear~~ year. My best regard to all. Did you get my picture if you didn't wridte to Mead Bros. Wood Stock Ill. Your truant son Ehrich Weiss." (Spelling and punctuation

11

as written.)

He hopped a train to make his way to Texas, but ended up in Kansas. He worked his way back up north. When he got word his father had moved to New York, Ehrich soon followed.

Houdini the athlete (Library of Congress)

Chapter Two
New York

AGAIN, THE family was left behind. Again, Samuel Weiss lived frugally to save the money needed to bring them to New York. And yet again, his income, mostly from tutoring to Hebrew students, was never enough. Ehrich contributed by working for two different companies as a messenger boy and assorted other odd jobs.

By 1888, they saved enough money to rent a cold-water flat and reunite the family. Their dark cloud followed from Milwaukee and dumped a once-in-a-lifetime blizzard on their new city, knocking down telephone poles and piling up thirty-foot snowdrifts. To heat the apartment, Samuel sold off some of his extensive theology library rather than take charity.

"We lived there, I mean we starved there, for several years," wrote Houdini.

There was also another mouth to feed, Cecilia gave birth to a daughter, Carrie Gladys (her actual birth year has thus far been impossible to discover and is argued to be anywhere between 1882 and 1891, in the 1930 census she listed her age as 38). While this added to the burden, Ehrich's brothers worked to add to the financial pool, Theo (Theodore, called "Dash" by the family) worked as a photographer's assistant.

There is some evidence that one of Ehrich's many odd jobs may have been for that same photographer. It was possibly Theo's boss who first taught Ehrich how to vanish a coin. The magic bug bit him.

He did continue with his athletic endeavors. A member of the Pastime Athletic Club, he took up boxing and only illness prevented him from competing for the 115 lb amateur championship. He had already beaten the eventual winner in an earlier bout. He took up long distance running defeating Sidney Thomas, an English champion, in a twenty-mile race. He set the speed record for a run around Central Park. Ehrich made life-long friends with the captain of the club, Joseph Rinn, who also shared an interest in magic and later became a valuable ally in Houdini's anti-spiritualism crusade.

Magic was becoming his passion.

Late that year, Ehrich started cutting the linings for men's ties for H. Richter & Sons in the garment district. Here he met Jacob Hyman, a boy a few years older and a fellow magic enthusiast. They shared tricks, mostly the card and coin effects they learned from the few magic books in print, like the classic teaching text, *Modern Magic* by

Professor Hoffman.

Ehrich practiced diligently. Private practice turned into public performance. Often alone as "Eric the Great," or partnered with Jacob, he began performing on a makeshift stage in the basement of his tenement building and at other neighborhood venues. To help his enthusiastic friend, the affluent Rinn, purchased some magic props from Martinka's magic shop as a gift to expand Ehrich's show.

With what little money he saved, Ehrich bought second hand magic books. His education was sparse, but he inherited a love of books and reading from his father. One afternoon he discovered the book that profoundly changed his life, *The Memoirs of Robert-Houdin, Ambassador, Author, and Conjuror, Written by Himself.*

Jean Eugene Robert-Houdin (1805-1871) is considered one of the greatest magicians of all time and the father of modern magic. He moved the art of magic away from using ornate lacquered boxes, unwieldy nickel-plated props, and heavy covered tables to more natural settings and sleight of hand. He abandoned the stories of the supernatural that made up the traditional magicians' patter and drew from current scientific themes instead.

The book reads like a grand adventure story. Robert-Houdin performed for royalty in his own theatre. He created and built intricate mechanical toys. As a clockmaker, his work is still highly collectable. Later in life, he experimented with electricity and automated his house with mechanical devices. He stopped a rebellion in Algiers with his magic; proving to the superstitious rebels that the French magic was greater than their magic and they made peace.

"My interest in conjuring and magic and my enthusiasm for Robert-Houdin came into existence simultaneously." Ehrich lost himself in the pages of the book and found a new self on the other side. He dedicated himself as never before, practicing four or five hours a day. "I accepted his writings as my text-book and my gospel."

Magic would now be his vocation as well as his avocation. "To my unsophisticated mind, his memoirs gave to the profession a dignity worth attaining at the cost of earnest, life-long effort."

Little did Ehrich Weiss realize his own biographies would likewise inspire the next generation of magicians.

Ehrich confided his desire to his friend Jacob, "I ask nothing more in life than to become in my profession like Robert-Houdin." Jacob told Ehrich that in the French language to add the letter "i" to the end of a person's name meant to be "like" that person. Houdin then became Houdini. Ehrich's nickname in the family was Ehrie, a virtual homophone of Harry. A name, in fact, he had already used while on the road.

Since they were to perform as partners, Jacob also changed his name, to J. H. Houdini. The act became "The

Brothers Houdini."

On April 3, 1891, Ehrich quit his job at Richter's, but before leaving got a recommendation letter on the advice of Joseph Rinn:

"To Whom It May Concern, We hereby certify that Mr. Ehrich Weiss has been in our employ for two years and six months as assistant lining cutter and we cheerfully recommend him as an honest, industrious young man."

At that moment, Ehrich Weiss took a last breath while Harry Houdini gasped his first.

Early promotional picture (Library of Congress)

Chapter Three
Struggling

"LADIES AND Gents, as youse can see I ain't got nothin' up my sleeve."

The Brothers Houdini weren't even ready for small-time show business. Their act was not an unpolished diamond, but a plain rock. Their props were threadbare. Their timing was a like a broken clock, correct only twice a day. They spoke in broken gutter English. It would be years before Harry would break his bad verbal habits. Bookings were slim. They performed when they could, often in Bowery saloons and beer halls for "throw money." There was the rare step up, like when Harry talked his way into performing at Huber's Dime Museum.

The dime museum's closest modern relative is the traveling sideshow. At one time, these were reasonably respectable establishments, but when the worlds of education and entertainment divorced, they moved into the low-class neighborhood.

In the dimes, there were two kinds of performers, the

freaks: giants, dwarves, armless men and women, the extremely fat, the skeleton skinny, and other human anomalies. Contrary to popular opinion, they were the stars of the show. They told a good story, made the most money, and lived a good life.

The other kind of performers were the working acts: strongmen, incombustible fire-eaters, sword-swallowers, blockheads, human pincushions, regurgitators, jugglers, and magicians. Most of these acts were has-beens, wanna-bes, and never-weres. Working acts were a commodity and paid accordingly.

At Huber's he met George Dexter, a master at rope-tie escapes. Dexter taught his secrets to an eager Houdini, fostering an interest in performing escapes. Houdini had a voracious appetite for knowledge. No matter where he performed, he sought out performers who would share their experience. He digested every lesson, every trick, every bit of advice and assimilated it all into his being. In the dime museums performing up to 20 shows a day there was plenty of time to put into practice his newfound knowledge.

Unfortunately, the bookers thought little of the future prospects of The Brothers Houdini and Jacob seemed to agree. Their partnership dissolved. The Brothers Houdini was short one brother. Luckily, Houdini was not. His younger brother Theo (Dash) joined the act.

Using Dash's savings, they purchased a retired

magician's props, including a steamer trunk designed for an escape trick. Around for over thirty years, the trunk trick was a moth eaten bit until inspiration struck Houdini.

Part of Houdini's genius was that he could take something that exists, give it a twist, and create something unique and startling.

An audience committee inspected the trunk and confirmed it free of gimmicks. Then they tied Houdini's hands tightly. Bound, they placed him in a just-large-enough canvas sack, which was also securely tied. The Houdini-filled sack went into the trunk. The committee padlocked the trunk and tied it all around with a spider web of ropes. Surrounding the trunk was a curtain with its front open to accept Dash. He stepped into the enclosure and just before shutting the curtains, he would say:

"Now I will clap my hands three times, and at the third and last time I ask you to watch CLOSELY!"

He rapidly closed the curtains. "CLAP." "CLAP." On the third "CLAP," the curtains flew open and there stood Houdini.

The trunk and bag were undone and Dash stood up, his arms bound just as Harry's arms had been, three seconds before. "Metamorphosis" shouted the brothers.

They closed their show with it.

The Metamorphosis was a great trick, a brilliant, stunning piece of magic. Countless modern magicians still perform it today. Yet the brothers made no progress towards fame and fortune.

The family also would have a setback. In September, Samuel Weiss became sick. He had cancer of the tongue, an ugly bleeding tumor, which required surgery. He never recovered. On October 5, 1892, he died. The death certificate listed "shock from surgery" as the cause. Cecilia, Houdini's mother, mourned her loss, "Weiss, Weiss, You have left me with your children. What have you done?"

Houdini recalled the oath given so many years before in Milwaukee. It was now more important than ever that he work to provide for his family.

In 1893, the brothers traveled to Chicago to appear at the World's Columbian Exposition. Not to perform in a theater as The Brothers Houdini, but along the Midway Plaisance, in dark make-up, performing magic and charming snakes as Hindu fakirs.

At the end of their run, Houdini picked up a solo spot at Kohl and Middleton's Clark St. Museum. This would be a valuable contact; throughout those lean years whenever Houdini was stuck, Mr. Hedges, the manager, could always find Harry a week's worth of work to save him from starvation.

Houdini left Chicago that summer with a new addition to his repertoire, The East Indian Needle Trick. He placed fifty or a hundred sharp steel sewing needles to his lips and appeared to chew and swallow them.

"You notice I swallow them eyes first, so they know where they're going," Houdini said.

Afterward a committee of spectators performed a near clinical examination of his mouth to confirm it was empty. He followed by swallowing yards of linen thread. His mouth again shown empty. Houdini cleared his throat, coughed, and pulled the end of the thread out of his mouth. Houdini continued to pull slowly until a needle was revealed hanging from the thread, then another needle, and another. He proceeded to regurgitate the entire length of linen with all the needles threaded on it.

These small improvements and additions were not enough. Something was still missing.

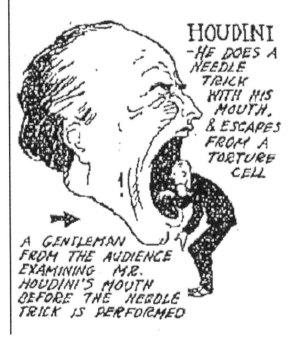

Cartoon featuring Houdini's Needle Trick
(*Chicago Tribune* 1924)

Chapter Four
Beatrice

THE SUMMER of 1894 found The Brothers Houdini performing at the Sea Beach Palace Hotel on Coney Island. One of the other acts on the bill was a song and dance trio, The Floral Sisters. Theo quickly arranged a double date with a couple of the "sisters."

Wilhelmina Beatrice Rahner was a petite brunette, less than five feet tall and around ninety pounds. Bess, as everyone called her, was a Brooklyn girl raised in a strict Roman Catholic family. At sixteen she ran away from home to be a seamstress in a traveling circus. A year later she convinced the two Floral Sisters to adopt a third.

The attraction was instant for Houdini. Dash may have seen her first, but Houdini always got his way. Within two weeks, Harry and Bess married in a civil service. She lent Houdini most of the money for the ring and even the two-dollar license fee. Harry was so poor those years later Bess would joke, "she married him for an orange." Just in case the first ceremony didn't take, there were two more, one by a rabbi and one by a Catholic priest. Contrary to popular opinion, Houdini's Jewish mother accepted the outsider into the family. Bess' Catholic mother, on the other hand, took over twelve years to accept the Jewish showman.

Houdini taught Bess the act. The petite Bess accomplished the exchange in the Metamorphosis in half the time it took Dash, making the trick all the more impressive. It was simple economics. The act could not support three people. The Brothers Houdini became The Houdinis.

At first, it was more of the same, dime museums and beer halls. However, within three months, The Houdinis secured a big-time vaudeville booking, Tony Pastor's Theater. They opened the week on the bottom of the bill.

Most of the audience never saw the opening performers. Opening acts often worked mute because no one was paying attention. They served as little more than "living wallpaper" as the audience arrived at the theater and settled in. Although, being at the bottom of the bill was sort of like being the ugliest girl in the Miss America pageant—at least you were on the same stage.

Half way through the week Tony Pastor moved their act up to fourth on the bill. Houdini had hoped this was their big break. He would be disappointed. They finished the week with no promise of a return engagement. Pastor's lukewarm single sentence recommendation didn't help. "The Houdinis' act as performed here I found satisfactory and interesting."

It was back to being "Dime Museum Harry." There, without Bess, he often appeared as "The King of Cards;" She refused to work in the deplorable conditions at some of the dime museums.

In 1895, The Houdinis joined up with the Welsh Brothers Circus. With potentially twenty-six weeks worth of work on the line, Houdini was ready for anything. He did Punch and Judy, a mind-reading act, magic, the trunk trick, and was in the parade. Bess assisted Harry and did her own song and dance number. The pay was "twenty-five a week and cakes." Cakes was circus talk for a room and meals.

There was another mysterious circus term on the contract concerning his duties: "and found." It meant you did whatever the boss found for you to do. Canvas needed to be put out, you pulled it. Stakes needed to be driven, you hammered. Projea, the Wild Man of Mexico is sick, you de-evolved.

At the end of the season, even after sending home half their salary, they had saved enough money to buy an interest in a burlesque company. It failed, the manager arrested for embezzlement.

Undeterred, Houdini kept moving forward, incorporating another element to their performances: handcuffs. First, he used them as a refinement to the Metamorphosis, then as publicity stunts, and later, as the rudiments of his future escape shows. He added a new wrinkle. He challenged the audience to bring their own restraints. He would defeat them all.

They joined the Marco Magic Company in Canada. It folded after playing to mostly empty houses because an inferior magician, also named Marco, had already burned up the territory.

Houdini picked up dates when and where he could to finish the Canadian season on his own. While touring in Nova Scotia, Harry obtained a straitjacket and experimented with escaping from it inside a curtained cabinet. The response was mild; aside from the popular trunk trick, he was just learning how to sell his escapes to the audience.

Late in 1897, they joined the California Concert Company, a medicine show. While still on the low rungs of show business, the years of struggle and the shear number of shows began to pay off. Soon Houdini's magic and escape act was the centerpiece of the show.

Desperate for money and needing to get around the blue laws that banned amusements on Sundays, Houdini and the troupe organized séances under the guise of religious services. Houdini recognized early on that spiritualist mediums were using magicians' techniques to make it appear as if they had contact with the dead. It was a simple transition and a huge hit. The local newspapers printed stories of The Houdinis' marvelous gifts. That one show brought in more money than the rest of the week's regular performances.

They continued to perform these "supernatural" feats after leaving the medicine show. The money was a great temptation. Despite that, in the end, Harry's moral code would not allow it. He became convinced that toying with people in such a fragile emotional state was immoral and the secret techniques they used bordered on the illegal. Proclaiming you can talk to the dead is engaging in a callous confidence game. He left that game to the flimflammers.

The Houdinis returned to magic. They also returned to the dime museums and circuses.

Harry was frustrated. For almost ten years—half of those with Bess—he had struggled and was still working the same old places, like Huber's and Kohl's. Later he wrote, "I contemplated quitting the show business, and retire to private life, meaning to work by day at one of my trades...and open a school of magic."

He did more than contemplate it. Houdini went to the newspapers and tried to sell the secrets of his handcuff act for twenty-five dollars. Nobody was willing to pay his price. He made a deal with a Chicago magic dealer, August Roterberg, to sell magic by mail. Like many of Houdini's other outside business ventures, it failed. He started a magic school, which got no more students than his father's Hebrew tutoring.

It may have been the lowest point in his life. A decision had to be made and Houdini made it. There would be one last tour. If they didn't find success? It would be quits.

The Houdinis and the Metamorphosis
(Library of Congress)

Chapter Five
Handcuffs

HOUDINI WAS back with the Welsh Brothers Circus, but this time something was different. His new Challenge Handcuff Act generated publicity. That publicity put bodies in the seats. The Welsh Brothers saw Houdini's growing popularity and offered his show as a separate "after show" attraction. For an extra fee, of course.

On January 5, 1899, while performing at Kohl and Middleton's Dime Museum, Houdini made the front page of the *Chicago Journal*. A reporter was loitering around the police station when in came this brash young man, boasting that he could release himself from any of their manacles.

The police had never seen anything like this crackpot. They thought they'd teach him a lesson. Laughing, they confidently trussed him up like a Christmas turkey. In half the time it took to restrain him, he escaped.

It appears from the article this all happened by coincidence. In fact, Houdini had schmoozed Detective Andy Rohan for several days, Bess regaling the officer with show business stories while Houdini examined the various restraints. Houdini brought in a reporter specifically to witness the event. The arranged story worked. Now, the audience came to the theater to see Houdini, not in spite of him.

Houdini discovered the alchemy of publicity. The name of the game was promotion. To sell tickets, get your name in the papers. To get your name in the papers, make friends with the reporters. The newspapermen just wanted a good story and good pictures. Houdini learned to give them both. Of course, the whiskey and sandwiches didn't hurt either.

Everywhere Houdini went, he combined those chemicals and the subsequent reaction made front-page news.

Now, being noticed brings trouble. Houdini challenged all comers. On January 13, Police Sergeant Waldron of Evanston, Illinois, slapped a pair of cuffs on him. Houdini retreated to his escape cabinet, a small curtained area on stage. Immediately, he was in trouble.

Most of the handcuffs of the time were simple locks. Generally, all the same make cuffs used the same key. Houdini had a duplicate of the key he needed, but it refused to budge. Waldron rigged the cuffs. Those cuffs were never going to open again. Humiliated, Houdini slunk off stage to have the cuffs sawed off.

He thought he was through. He expected Hedges to fire him. Instead, the manager of Kohl's, brushed it off, "it could happen to anybody." Only one paper commented briefly and the reporter actually chided Waldron for not playing fair. Life went on, but a valuable lesson was learned, control the situation, prepare ahead of time and make them lock and unlock the cuffs *before* you put them on.

In March, he received a telegram that changed the journey of his life forever.

Chicago, Mar. 14 '99

Houdini, You can open Omaha Mar. 26. $60. Will see act. Probably make you proposition all next season.

[signed] M. Beck.

Martin Beck was the most powerful theatrical agent in the world. He booked the Orpheum circuit. The Orpheum owned the majority of vaudeville houses west of the Mississippi river. Partnered with the Keith circuit in the east, they controlled big-time vaudeville. This was everything he and Bess had worked for. This would mean continuous work and more money than ever. Sixty dollars a week! At the time, bread was only three cents a loaf.

Martin Beck discovered Houdini performing in St. Paul, Minnesota. He recognized a flaw in Houdini's act. He thought Houdini used fake handcuffs. Houdini was not the first magician to escape from cuffs, but most used their own-

gimmicked equipment. However, when Beck saw the "Challenge Act" and when Houdini escaped from his cuffs, he was convinced he found a new novelty.

Harry was now the diamond, one that still needed some polish, but a diamond nevertheless. Beck advised Houdini to drop the magic and only perform the needles, the cuffs, and the trunk trick.

Beck stopped billing the act as The Houdinis. It became Harry Houdini or Houdini. He tried out various appellations, such as The Wizard of the Shackles, The King of Handcuffs, or, my favorite, The Celebrated Police Baffler. Bess' billing dropped to assistant; mostly she was not even billed at all. Except for the trunk trick, her role in the show was relegated to mostly standing off to the side of the stage looking worried.

Houdini and Bess worked their way west. As positive reports of the act's success poured into Martin Beck's office, he raised Houdini's weekly salary to $90, and then $125. By the time he performed his first jail cell escape in Los Angeles, it had ballooned to $400 a week. (To put this in some perspective, the average *yearly* family budget in 1899 was $490.)

The jail cell escape added to the impossibility of his publicity stunts. He would be heavily manacled as before and then placed in a locked prison cell. To the dismay of his jailers, he still escaped. For the public, this was spectacular.

Now, being noticed brings exposure. In one Los Angeles newspaper, an article appeared purporting to expose all of Houdini's secret methods. The article said that Houdini simply carried duplicate keys to the locks all over his person. Was it true? No.

"The more they write the more they'll come to see you," Martin Beck said as he told Harry to ignore it.

Instead, Houdini ignored Beck's advice and fought back. He maintained that the police had completely examined his person before the attempt and found no keys. To prove it, he returned to the jail with reporters in tow. He insisted that this time they strip him naked and he would nevertheless still escape. He did.

At a time when Victorian prudery prevented the word "naked" to be printed in some newspapers, Houdini upped the ante. His act was something new, exotic, something people would pay for. His semi-nude picture on any newspaper's front page helped boost the circulation, as well.

The audiences in the west enthusiastically embraced Houdini, but the audiences in the east still kept him at arms length. He clashed with Martin Beck. Houdini was always the boss and he chaffed with having to answer to Beck. He blamed the reception on bad bookings by Beck. He resented Beck's 15% to 20% commission. He felt there would be better prospects in Europe.

On May 26, 1900, Harry filled out his first passport. On

the line for birthplace he correctly wrote in, Buda-Pest. He applied for a subsequent passport, just a few months later, and on that application his birthplace magically changed to Appleton. His height would also change through the years from 5' 6" on his first passport to 5' 7" on his second and 5' 9" on the third.

Houdini was deleting the story that was and creating the story he wanted to be, erasing away the old Ehrich Weiss as best he could.

The Houdinis at Kohl & Middleton's Museum
(*Chicago Tribune* 1896)

Chapter Six
England

HOUDINI ONLY ever feared one thing: sea travel. Even standing on the dock, with the thought of going on a boat set his stomach churning. The voyage from New York to England was rough sailing. Bess said she had to tie the Escape King to his bunk out of fear he might make good his threats to jump overboard and end his suffering.

This may have been another Houdini exaggeration. While he did suffer from seasickness, he was not too sick to perform a couple of shows on the voyage. Something he did on every "nauseating" boat trip he took.

In London, Harry's anger at Martin Beck boiled over. He went expecting contracts. There were none. He broke away from Beck. They would forever remain friends and when Houdini needed advice, it was to Beck he would turn, but their business relationship was over.

Houdini hired his own agent, Harry Day, to handle the bookings. They finally met with the manager of the Alhambra, C. Dundas Slater.

The Alhambra was one of the top vaudeville houses in the United Kingdom. Houdini showed off his press book from America, articles on his escapes and glowing reviews. Slater was dubious. This attitude was the same everywhere Houdini tried to interview for a job. The English thought the American newspapers and police were untrustworthy. They both were too easily bribed.

Slater offered a challenge of his own, if Houdini escaped Scotland Yard's shackles, then he would believe. It was the challenge Houdini had longed for.

Slater, Day, and Houdini entered the Scotland Yard office of Police Inspector William Melville and explained the situation. "If he can get out of your cuffs," Slater said, "he's got a job waiting for him."

Melville replied, "Mr. Slater, but you realize these darbies are not stage handcuffs."

He pulled out a pair of cuffs.

"Follow me." He led the men out into the hallway and stopped next to a pillar. "Here's how we fasten Yankee criminals who come over here and make trouble," Melville said. He made Houdini hug the pillar and then he snapped the cuffs on, trapping Houdini's arms around the pillar.

"I'm going to leave you here while we go out for lunch," Melville laughed. "We'll be back for you in a couple of hours."

They turned toward the door and heard the clatter of

metal hitting the floor.

"Wait, I'll go with you. Here's the way a Yankee gets out of your handcuffs." Houdini walked away from the pillar, free.

The run at the Alhambra started with a bang. Houdini's name was on the lips of every Englishmen and a visit to Houdini backstage became a must for London society. While the rest of England begged to see Houdini, his engagement was extended for six more weeks as he set new box office records.

Capitalizing on the "Houdini mania," he undertook a tour of English music halls.

While performing in Sheffield, Houdini escaped from the prison cell that held Charles Peace, a notorious murderer. Coupling his star to the infamous multiplied the impact and press coverage, a practice he would repeat in other cities.

As fast as his fame spread, so did the word that allowing Houdini to escape your gaol was an embarrassment for the police. He found it increasingly difficult to promote the show. Even bribes no longer worked.

He created a new challenge, the Packing Case Escape. Going into a town, he would arrange to have a wooden shipping crate built by a local business. With community pride on the line and the free advertising by the business, the theaters were standing room only.

In Glasgow, people were rioting to get seats. Ticket

prices were doubled and temporary bleachers were built on the stage to accommodate the throng. The local carpenters built a heavy packing case right on the stage and nailed Houdini into it. After the escape, Houdini wrote in his diary, "Mob waited for me. Took me shoulder high, carried me home and upstairs. Had to make speech from the window."

Houdini offered twenty-five pounds to anyone who could cuff him so that he could not escape. Not all challenges were easy. In Blackburn, strongman William Hodgson brought on six pairs of heavy irons, chains, and padlocks. Houdini refused. He noted the locks appeared to be tampered with. The audience turned against him. Against his better judgment, he went on with the challenge.

Hodgson torturously fettered Houdini, at one time so viciously wrenching his arms that Houdini complained that, "it was no part of the challenge that his arms should be broken." On his knees, hog-tied, in great agony, his arms turning black and blue, they placed him in the curtained escape cabinet and he began his attempt. The orchestra played.

After twenty minutes, the curtain was opened. Houdini lay on his side. They feared he had fainted. When he requested to be put upright, Hodgson refused. The audience booed and hissed. Houdini's brother Dash pushed Hodgson aside and lifted him into place.

Another fifteen minutes passed, Houdini asked the chains

be loosened for a moment because his hands had become numb. Hodgson refused to more catcalls.

"This is a bet, not a love match," he said. "If you are beaten, give in."

The doctor on hand thought it cruel to keep him chained any longer. Houdini refused to quit. Cheers erupted.

Fifteen more minutes. Houdini raised one hand over the curtain. It was free. The rest of Houdini still bound tight. He rested for a moment.

Someone in the crowd yelled for him to give up. Another voice countered, "Keep going." He begged the audience for more patience, again, reminding them that Hodgson tampered with the locks. Houdini won the spectators' sympathy and they turned on Hodgson. A police sergeant watching the proceedings suggested that for his own safety Hodgson should leave.

A few minutes later, Houdini's second hand was free.

At ten minutes to twelve, nearly two hours after it had begun; the curtains of the cabinet flew open. Houdini was free. He staggered out, his shirt torn from waist to collar, blood dripped from his wrists. The audience cheered for fifteen minutes.

Houdini spoke, "Ladies and Gentlemen, I have been in the handcuff business for fourteen years, but never have I been so brutally and cruelly ill-treated. I would just like to say again that the locks were plugged."

The audience streamed out of the theater to yells of, "Where's Hodgson?"

Harry carried that night with him until his death. Two years later a reporter wrote, "I noticed on Houdini's arms several scars, as though some tiger had clawed him."

Houdini chained (Library of Congress)

Chapter Seven
Germany and Russia

HOUDINI ALTERNATED his tours of the English theaters with tours in other countries, mostly Germany. Before he was allowed perform, the German police had to certify his act. Under the rule of Emperor Wilhelm II, Germany was an authoritarian state. The police had the power to censor and approve all forms of entertainment. Houdini won approval, but that could be revoked at any time.

Houdini surprised and delighted his German audiences by speaking their language in his performances. They didn't know that the elusive American spoke German at home. The shows were sell-outs, hundreds of people turned away each night.

Much has been written about Houdini as a symbol. He was a self-liberator. He embodied the struggles of his fans trying to free themselves from the old world shackles. This deep appeal must have been especially evident in the Germany of the Kaiser, where almost everything not compulsory was *verboten*. Openly defying the police was a dangerous game.

Houdini experienced several arduous challenges. One so damaged his wrists he could not put handcuffs on for a week. In another, a particularly torturous set of thumb cuffs tore strips of flesh from his thumbs. The German restraints more resembled the torture devices of the Inquisition than the tools of law enforcement.

He added a cog to his publicity machine, The Bridge Jump. Handcuffed, wrapped with chains, and padlocked, he leapt into the river and stayed submerged until the crowd thought he had drowned. Suddenly, he broke the surface, unfettered, holding the restraints aloft. When he got ashore, the *Schutzmann* (the constable) arrested him. As there was no law against jumping into the river, the court fined him fifty cents for walking on the grass.

There were more significant legal troubles. In a newspaper, policeman Werner Graff accused Houdini of being a "fraud," that Houdini was "misrepresenting his talents" and the German people needed to be protected from him. The charges had serious implications.

Houdini sued for slander. During the trial, Graff explained that the American could only release himself from his own manacles, since everyone knew that it was impossible for criminals to escape such devices placed upon them by the duly appointed officers of the *Reich*.

Houdini's lawyer turned this around into a challenge. An officer locked Houdini in a regulation wrist chain and padlock. He slipped it easily. The court found for the plaintiff. Graff was ordered to apologize.

Graff appealed. He had a specifically designed "un-openable" lock. Houdini opened it. The higher court ruled again in his favor.

Graff appealed again, this time to the highest court in the land. The five judges sided with Houdini. Graff was fined thirty marks, paid all court costs, and had to apologize publicly "in the name of the Kaiser." Additionally, Houdini could publish the verdict in the Cologne newspapers, at Graff's expense.

The public's enthusiasm turned to hysteria.

While Germany provided Houdini with bureaucratic difficulties, his next stop, Russia, where the pogroms (what is now charmingly called ethnic cleansing) slaughtered untold numbers of Jews, would prove to be his most sinister challenge yet.

From the moment he entered the country it started. At the border his papers were confiscated, his bags ransacked, and he was charged a duty on his professional equipment. The Russian police kept him under surveillance at all times.

Czarist Russian was out of step with the rest of the Europe. The locks so crude, the jails so miserable, Houdini had to find a new escape to arouse the public's interest. The chief of the Russian Secret Police gave him the answer. It was the Siberian Transport Cell.

To the outsider it looked impregnable, to the insider it was. A steel safe on wheels, this was the vehicle used to convey Russia's most dangerous criminals to confinement in Siberia. The zinc-lined cabinet had a single door with a barred window two feet above the lock, which was welded to the outside of the door. Once the key secured the special lock, only a second different key opened it. That second key was twenty-one miles away.

Houdini stripped and endured an exhaustive examination not once or twice, but three times. His assistant, Franz Kukol was also subjected to a thorough frisking.

Once Houdini was locked inside, the van was moved, its back to a wall, so he could work in private. He made short work of the handcuffs. Twenty-eight minutes later the door swung open. The police were enraged. They grabbed

Houdini and his assistant, then forced them to endure another grueling inspection. They refused to let him advertise his escape, but the word spread anyway.

Houdini later wrote a friend, "What a searching. Three secret police, or what we would call spies, searched me one after the other, and talk about getting the finger, well I received it three times, but Mr. Russian Spy found nothing."

Houdini made tremendous amounts of money in Russia, but found little to like. "After you leave Russia, you feel as if you had yourself come out of some sort of mild prison." He never returned.

Houdini's first big success in Chicago
(*Chicago Tribune* 1899)

Chapter Eight
The Mirror Cuffs

"ARE THERE any challengers?"

Houdini and the audience watched as a smartly dressed man made his way up to the stage at London's Hippodrome. He held an odd pair of handcuffs. They were unusually heavy, with a single cuff that fastened both wrists. The lock was made of two Bramah locks, one nested inside the other. The distinctive key was six inches long.

Houdini refused them. He specified *regulation* cuffs in his public challenges. These were not regulation.

The man spoke to the audience, "On behalf of my newspaper, *The Daily Mirror*, I have just challenged Mr. Houdini to permit me to fasten these handcuffs on his wrists. Mr. Houdini declines. In the course of my journalistic duties, this week I interviewed a blacksmith at Birmingham named Nathaniel Hart who has spent five years of his life perfecting a lock, which he alleges no mortal man can pick. The handcuff I wish to fasten upon Mr. Houdini contains such a lock. The key alone took a week to make. The handcuffs are made of the finest British steel, by a British workman, and being property of *The Daily Mirror,* have been bought with British gold. Mr. Houdini is evidently afraid of British-made handcuffs, for will not put on this pair."

Houdini was at a loss for words.

"Now Mr. Houdini, you claim to be the 'Handcuff King.'

Everywhere I see huge posters of your feats. If you again refuse to put on the cuffs, you are no longer entitled to use the words 'Handcuff King.'"

Houdini was cornered. "I cannot possibly accept this challenge tonight, because I am restricted to time. His handcuffs, he admits, have taken five years to make. I know I can't get out of them in five minutes. There is not one lock in those cuffs, but a half dozen or more. I will make a match if the management will allow a special matinee for the purposes. It will take me a long time to get out, even if I can do so."

The special matinee was set for March 17, 1904. The next day, *The Daily Mirror* reported on the event:

Not a seat was vacant in the mighty Hippodrome yesterday afternoon when Harry Houdini, the "Handcuff King," stepped into the arena and received an ovation worthy of a monarch.

For days past all London has been aware that on Saturday night last a representative of the *Mirror* had stepped into the arena, in response to Houdini's challenge to anybody to come forward and successfully manacle him, and had there and then made a match with America's Mysteriarch for Thursday afternoon.

In his travels, the journalist had encountered a Birmingham blacksmith who spent five years of his life in devising a lock, which, he alleged, "no mortal man could pick." Promptly seeing he was in touch with a good thing, the press man had at once put an option upon the handcuffs, containing this lock and brought it back to London with him.

It was submitted to London's best locksmiths, who were unanimous in their admiration of it, asserting that in all their experience they had never before seen such a wonderful mechanism.

As a result, the editors of the *Mirror* determined to put the locks to the severest test possible by challenging Mr. Houdini to be manacled with the cuffs.

Like a true sportsman, Mr. Houdini accepted our challenge in the spirit in which it was given, although, on his own confession, he did not like the look of the lock.

MIGHTY AUDIENCE

Mr. Houdini's call was for three o'clock yesterday, but so intense was the excitement that the 4,000 spectators present could scarcely restrain their impatience whilst the six excellent turns which preceded him.

Waiting quietly and unnoticed by the arena steps, the *Mirror* representative watched Mr. Houdini's entrance and joined in giving his opponent-to-be in the lists one of the finest ovations mortal man has ever received.

"I am ready," said Houdini, concluding his address to the audience, "to be manacled by the *Mirror* representative if he is present."

A hearty burst of applause greeted the journalist as he stepped into the arena and shook hands with the "Handcuff King."

Then, in the fewest words possible, the press man called for volunteers from the audience to act upon a committee to see fair play, and Mr. Houdini asked his friends also to step into the arena and watch his interests.

HOUDINI HANDCUFFED
This done, the journalist placed the handcuffs on Mr. Houdini's wrists and snapped them. Then, with an effort, he turned the key six times, thus securing the bolt as firmly as possible.

The committee being satisfied as to the security of the handcuff, Mr. Houdini said;-- "*Ladies and Gentlemen:*--I am now locked up in a handcuff that has taken a British mechanic five years to make. I do not know whether I am going to get out of it or not, but I can assure you I am going to do my best."

Applauded to the echo, the Mysteriarch then retired within the cabinet that contains so many of his secrets.

All chronometers chronicled 3:15.

In a long line in front of the stage stood the committee. Before them, in the center of the arena, stood the little cabinet Houdini loves to call his "ghost house." Restlessly pacing to and fro, the *Mirror* representative kept an anxious eye on it.

FALSE HOPE OVERTHROWN
Those who have never stood in the position of

a challenger can scarcely realize the sense of responsibility felt by one who has openly thrown down the gauntlet to a man who is popular with the public.

The *Mirror* had placed its reliance on the work of a British mechanic, and if Houdini succeeded in escaping in the first few minutes it was felt that the proceedings would develop into a mere farce.

But time went by; 5, 10, 15, 20 minutes sped. Still the band played on. Then, at 22 minutes, Mr. Houdini put his head out of the cabinet "ghost house" and this was the signal for a great outburst of cheering.

"He is free! He is free!" shouted several; and universal disappointment was felt when it was ascertained that he had only put his head outside the cabinet in order to get a good look at the lock in strong electric light.

The band broke into a dreamy waltz as Houdini once more disappeared within the canopy. The disappointed spectators looked at their watches, murmured, "What a shame!" gave Houdini an encouraging clap, and the journalist resumed his stride.

At 35 minutes, Mr. Houdini again emerged. His collar was broken, water trickled in great channels down his face, and he looked generally warm and uncomfortable.

"My knees hurt," he explained to the audience. "I am not done yet."

The "house" went frantic with delight at their favorite's resolve, and this suggested an idea to the *Mirror* representative.

He spoke rapidly to Mr. Parker, the Hippodrome manager, who was at the side of the stalls. The gentleman looked thoughtful for a moment, then nodded his head and whispered something to an attendant.

A WELCOME CONCESSION

Presently the man appeared bearing a large cushion.

"The *Mirror* has no desire to submit Mr. Houdini to a torture test," said the representative, "and if Mr. Houdini will permit me, I shall have great pleasure in offering him the use of this cushion."

The "Handcuff King" was glad evidently of the rest for his knees, for he pulled it through into the "ghost house."

Ladies trembled with suppressed excitement, and, despite the weary wait, not a yawn was noticed throughout the vast audience. For 20 minutes, more the band played on, and then Houdini was seen to emerge once more from the cabinet.

Still handcuffed!

Almost a moan broke over the vast assemblage as this was noticed. He looked about for a moment, and then advanced to where his challenger stood.

"Will you remove the handcuffs for a moment," he said, "in order that I may take my coat off?"

For a few seconds the journalist considered. Then he replied: "I am indeed sorry to disoblige you, Mr. Houdini, but I cannot unlock those cuffs unless you admit you are defeated."

The reason was obvious. Mr. Houdini had seen the cuffs locked, but he had never seen them unlocked. Consequently, the press man thought there might be more in the request than appeared on the surface.

FROCK COAT SACRIFICED

Houdini evidently does not stick at trifles. He maneuvered until he got a pen knife from his waistcoat pocket. This he opened with his teeth, and then, turning his coat inside out over his head, calmly proceeded to cut it to pieces.

The novelty of the proceeding delighted the audience, who yelled themselves frantic. The *Mirror* representative had a rather warm five minutes of it at this juncture. Many of the audience did not see the reason, and expressed their disapproval of his action loudly.

Grimly, however, he looked on and watched Mr. Houdini once more re-enter the cabinet. Time sped on, and presently somebody recorded that the Mysteriarch had been manacled just one hour. Ten minutes more of anxious waiting, and then a surprise was in store for everybody.

VICTORY

The band just finished a stirring march when,

with a great shout of victory, Houdini bounded from the cabinet holding the shining handcuffs in his hand—free!

A mighty roar of gladness went up. Men waved their hats, shook hands with the other. Ladies waved their handkerchiefs, and the committee, rushing forward as one man, shouldered Houdini, and bore him in triumph around the arena.

But the strain had been too much for the "Handcuff King." And he sobbed as though his heart would break.

With a mighty effort, however, he regained his composure, and received the congratulations of the *Mirror* in the true sportsmanlike spirit he had shown throughout the contest.

A SPORTMAN'S TELEGRAM

Last night Mr. Houdini sent us the following telegram:--

"Allow me to thank you for the open and upright manner in which your representative treated me in today's contest. Must say that it was one of the hardest, but at the same time one of the fairest tests I ever had."

The story of Houdini escaping the *Mirror* cuffs made every paper in England. London alone had over thirty daily papers. Houdini broke all the box office records he set on his earlier visits to London. Days later, the *Mirror* presented Houdini with a sterling silver replica of the cuffs he had escaped.

Over the years, there have been many erroneous theories as to how Houdini accomplished the feat. It wasn't until William Kalush revealed the research of Houdini expert Bill Liles in his book, *The Secret Life of Houdini* that we had the truth. Normally, I would not reveal any secrets, but this was a one time only event and it sheds more light on the real genius of Houdini.

Bill Liles had the opportunity to examine both the original cuffs and the silver presentation replica. What he found changed everything we've thought for over a century.

First, the cuffs he escaped from were not adjustable, therefore they had to fit Houdini perfectly, or the escape would not have been possible. How did the Birmingham blacksmith Nathaniel Hart know Houdini's wrist size? Also, why would he work five years on an unpickable handcuff lock when most experts thought the restraints of the time were more than adequate? Houdini had only been showing the world otherwise for less than four years.

Second, The silver replica presentation cuffs: By law, every silver item made in England carries a mark. The mark on the presentation cuffs indicates they might have been made months before the challenge. Yet, at the show, the *Mirror* representative said they *would* be made. Excusing the reporter's phrasing as a slip of the tongue, how did they know they would need a silver presentation copy to give as a prize before there was even the thought of a challenge? Equally telling, they presented the cuffs to Houdini only a few days after the event. Could it take only a few days to duplicate, in silver, the handcuffs it took five years to construct?

Last, Liles found no evidence that the Birmingham blacksmith, Nathaniel Hart, ever existed.

It is clear now that Houdini conspired with the *Mirror* to orchestrate a brilliant drama, played out as real life.

The *Mirror* won with greater circulation. The people won because they experienced the birth of a legend first hand. Houdini won because he would forever after be the world's only King of the Handcuffs.

With his supreme triumph in London, Houdini finished off the last of his tour in Scotland. He had put off America for five years until he received the telegram he was waiting for. The one offering him a $1000 a week.

Houdini river jump, Harvard Bridge,
Boston, Massachusetts 1908
(Library of Congress)

56

Chapter Nine
Rivals

"FOR YEARS there has not been such a sensation as Houdini," the *Chicago Daily News* reported. "His coming into the ranks of vaudeville brings a new light which is not likely to be extinguished by the army of imitators, of apes, of envious fakers."

Houdini created a completely new genre of magic, seemingly overnight, with the Challenge Handcuff and Escape Act, and by the next morning, there were dozens of would-be handcuff kings. Harry thought the way to deal with such offenses was to fight.

Many stole Houdini's name outright, a few, at least, changing the spelling. His old partner, Jacob Hyman laid claim to the Houdini name. For over eight years after the break up, he performed under one variation of Houdini or another. If anyone had a right to use the Houdini name, Jacob did, but Harry still felt it wasn't right and never forgave him.

With others, Houdini would attack ruthlessly.

In Germany, the "Handcuff Champion of Handcuff Champions" Kleppini boasted from the stage nightly that not only had he escaped from Houdini's handcuffs but also Kleppini's own manacles had defeated the great Houdini.

Houdini was touring Holland when he received a message about the pretender. Fuming, Houdini took a leave of absence and sped to Dortmund to confront Kleppini.

Disguised as an old man, Houdini waited in the audience for Kleppini to begin. When his rival claimed to have defeated Houdini, he stood up and yelled, "Not true."

"How would you know?" Kleppini replied.

"I am in the know." Houdini said.

"Would you like to wager that I am telling the truth?" Kleppini was surprised as the old man bounded onto the stage.

"You say I am not telling the truth," Houdini ripped off his disguise. "I know, because, I am Houdini!"

Houdini handed Kleppini a pair of handcuffs and offered him five thousand German marks if he could escape. After much haggling between Kleppini, his manager, and Houdini, Kleppini refused. Houdini reluctantly stalked back to his seat, fuming. Much of the audience left the theater, disgusted by Kleppini's false advertising.

The next day, Herr Reutter, the manager of the theater, negotiated a deal that would be agreeable to Houdini. Instead of Houdini challenging Kleppini, they would advertise that Kleppini had challenged Houdini to the contest.

Before leaving, Herr Reutter asked to examine the cuffs Houdini would use. Houdini presented several, but one in particular caught the manager's eye. Houdini explained they were French letter cuffs. The cuffs had an unusual cylinder combination lock using letters instead of numbers. By rotating the five cylinders to form a word, it unlocked. Houdini spun the letters to spell *clefs*, the French word for keys and the cuffs opened.

The evening of the challenge, Houdini offered the choice of handcuffs to Kleppini. He was hardly surprised when Kleppini chose the letter cuffs. Immediately Kleppini ran to the privacy of his escape cabinet.

"Ladies and gentlemen," Houdini shouted. "Do not let him tell you that the cuffs have been locked. They are open."

Kleppini came out from behind the curtains. "I will open these cuffs."

Houdini knew that Kleppini double-checked the cuffs to make sure that *clefs* still opened them. Kleppini insisted he be shackled immediately. Houdini had another plan.

Houdini wrestled with Kleppini, pushing this way, pulling that way, all around the stage until he finally locked the handcuffs.

With a look of disdain toward Houdini, Kleppini ducked into his cabinet.

"Ladies and gentlemen, you can all go home," Houdini laughed.

Kleppini started his escape attempt at nine o'clock. By nine-thirty, the cabinet was moved aside to allow a ballet act to perform. By eleven, most of the spectators had gone home. Kleppini was no nearer to getting out than when he started. At one in the morning, the manager ordered Kleppini to give up.

With the manager and, more importantly, a reporter watching, Houdini turned the cylinders to unlock the handcuffs. The cuffs sprung open when the letters F-R-A-U-D clicked into place. During his on stage tussle with Kleppini, Houdini had changed the combination.

Houdini disrupted or disposed these copycat Houdinis in a variety of ways. Sometimes upon receiving one of Houdini's cease and desist letters, the offending magician would do both. If not, Houdini verbally attacked in the press and on stage. In Europe, where he could copyright his act, he handled the matter in court. Other times, Houdini, or one of his brothers would go to rivals' shows with special handcuffs that, once locked, could never be opened, only sawed off. There are a few documented instances that they used violence to intimidate an imposter.

However, Houdini's most effective defense would be a rival of his own creation.

Houdini visits with Chicago magic dealer
August Roterberg and his wife between
1912-1916
(Library of Congress)

Chapter Ten
Hardeen

WHILE IN Berlin, Houdini sent a cable to New York, "Dash, Come over. The apples are ripe." By the time his brother arrived, Houdini had an entire duplicate of his escape act built and theater dates waiting to be filled. He even selected a new performing name for his younger brother: Hardeen.

Hardeen was the perfect choice to run interference for Houdini with other rivals. His friends would describe him as a "harum-scarum, hell-raisin' boy," who could "fight like a wildcat." He was bigger, tougher, and more cynical than Houdini.

Houdini had Hardeen booked by a rival circuit. Sometimes Houdini would follow Hardeen into a town and top his performances. When they were booked at the same time in the same town, Houdini performed in the largest theater, Hardeen the next largest. This strategy successfully shut out any other escape acts.

Never hiding the fact they were brothers, they trumped up a rivalry, playing out a war of words in the newspapers. The resultant publicity filled both theaters. However, at times, a real feud replaced the fake one, especially when Hardeen was quoted by a newspaper that he "so much admired Houdini that he was willing to hire him as an assistant." Houdini's ego bruised further when, in Europe,

Hardeen would prove to be every bit Houdini's equal. Some reviewers even preferred the faster paced act of Hardeen to his more methodical brother. Whatever hurts inflicted, real or imagined, a private apology by Dash always restored their brotherly bonds.

Hardeen relished the business, "the newspapers have us cutting each other's throats and us just two loving brothers living off the fat of the land."

Hardeen also altered the escape act in significant ways, especially the straitjacket release. First, to clear up a common misconception, it is not a "*straight* jacket." The word "strait" means tight or narrow.

It was used to restrain the murderously insane, to keep them from hurting another person or harming themselves. The jacket was designed for one thing and only one thing: to keep someone from getting out.

Another misconception is that to gain enough slack to accomplish the escape, Houdini needed to dislocate his shoulder. From my own experience, this is not only impossible, but unnecessary.

While Houdini pioneered the straitjacket escape, Hardeen discovered its greatest dramatic potential. While performing in Wales, two constables strapped him in and placed him in the ever-present escape cabinet. One of the officers tried to peek inside, an assistant pulled him away.

Time dragged on and the audience became impatient. After fifteen minutes, Dash released himself. Few in the audience applauded. The constable expressed what the audience was thinking. He didn't believe Hardeen could escape without outside help. He challenged him to repeat the test.

This was trouble. No one believed he had escaped, but

he was too exhausted to be strapped in a second time. He'd never get out. Being a smart businessman, he countered that if they returned in two nights he would free himself—*in full view of the audience.* This special show would necessitate another round of ticket sales.

Every seat in the theater was filled when Hardeen was strapped in the restraint jacket. As they finished pulling his arms tight and buckling them behind him, Hardeen said he would expect an apology when he slipped free. The crowd cheered him.

Hardeen began to struggle, first kneeling, and then rolling on the stage. He twisted and turned. The audience squirmed, involuntarily acting out his struggle in their seats. He forced his bound arms over his head and worked the buckles through the heavy canvas. The audience went wild. He wiggled and wormed the jacket over his head and off as the crowd leapt to their feet with a mighty roar.

Two days later Hardeen sent the newspaper articles to his brother. Impressed, Houdini immediately adopted the stunt. It was a success. Through the years, hundreds of thousands of people would crowd the streets to see Houdini. Adding to the danger, he performed the escape hanging upside down, in the open air, off the side of a building…a building that just happened to house the town's newspaper offices.

Hardeen promotional poster issued after Houdini's death
(Library of Congress)

Chapter Eleven
Home

BEFORE HE departed Scotland in 1904, Houdini made a farewell speech after his last show. He was leaving for America. He told the audience it had been five years since he last performed on his native soil. The audience sent him offstage with three rousing cheers. After changing his clothes and packing up the show, he left the theater. His fans, still waiting, crowded the alley behind the building. Several hoisted him up on their shoulders and carried him through the town to the railway station. Others in the parade of well-wishers sang—"And when ye go, will ye nae come back?"

Houdini, moved by the demonstration, "wept like a child."

After his triumphs in Europe, he expected to come home to a hero's welcome, but he was sorely disappointed. Yes, he got the salary he demanded, but, in America, getting fame was another thing entirely. He had to make his name all over again. Other than the readers of the trade papers, who published Houdini's near daily reports of his European successes, the public did not know the name Houdini.

That needed to change.

Houdini leapt into his routine of publicity stunts: jail escapes and bridge jumps.

His escape from the United States Jail in Washington D. C., January 6, 1906, had all the elements of a good press story. The cells were stone structures with heavy oak doors sunk into the walls three feet from the face of the corridor wall. When the door was shut, an L-shaped bar angled out and to the right where it tripped a steel catch that engaged the lock. Once engaged, the lock could only be opened with a key. Every cell used the same key. Houdini agreed to attempt an escape from Cell Number 2, the same specially reinforced vault that once held Charles J. Guiteau, the assassin of President James A. Garfield.

Harry was "stripped stark naked," thoroughly searched by the prison doctor, and thrown into the cell. The bizarre sight shocked Walter Hamilton, the current resident of the cell, awaiting the gallows for smothering his wife. He crouched in the corner in fear as it took Houdini two minutes to work his way out.

Then, uncharacteristically, straight-as-an-arrow Houdini engaged in some devilish mischief. He quickly opened all the cells on "Murderer's Row." The inmates, surprised by the naked escapologist, meekly followed orders as Houdini shuffled them from one room to the next.

With all the prisoners arranged in different cells, Houdini dressed and walked into the room holding the waiting group of dignitaries and reporters. Twenty-six minutes after being locked in, he completed his adventure.

As he sauntered in, he announced, "I let all your prisoners out." He let the thought sink in.

Two guards jumped up and ran to the door.

"But I locked them up again," added Houdini.

It was his most thrilling stunt to date and a publicity boon.

Through the years one of his most talked about stunts was his jump from the Bell Isle Bridge in Detroit, Michigan on November 27, 1906. He would repeatedly tell the story to reporters. It was the centerpiece of his posthumous biography written by Harold Kellock, and famously depicted in the popular 1953 Tony Curtis movie, *Houdini*.

Houdini prepared for the frigid waters by submerging himself in a bathtub filled with chunks of ice. His practice routine alone made for chilling headlines.

The day of the jump, the river was frozen over. Not to be deterred, Houdini ordered a hole chopped through the thick ice.

While stripping down to his bathing suit, he stopped, took an envelope from his pocket, and hastily wrote a will. He handed it to his assistant, Jim Collins, for safekeeping. It read simply, "I leave all to Bess."

Houdini—handcuffed and chained with heavy leg irons—leaped into the swift-running river through the hole. A few thousand shivering people watched the breach for any sign their hero.

One minute passed.

Two minutes.

Three.

At four minutes, the police gave up hope.

At the end of five, the half-frozen reporters ran to file their stories.

At eight, one of his assistants was stopped from jumping in to search for him.

The spectators slowly scattered. Bess, waiting nervously for hours back at the hotel, heard a newsboy yell, "Houdini dead." A moment later, Houdini walked through the door.

Houdini said that the strong current pulled him away from the hole and he could not find it. Refusing to panic, he took breaths of air trapped in the spaces between the water and ice. Then, he swam in ever widening circles until he found a fracture in the ice that led to the surface.

The only problem, it wasn't true.

The late Robert Lund, a devoted magic historian and founder of the American Museum of Magic, tracked down the original newspaper article from the *Detroit News.*

"HANDCUFF KING" JUMPS MANACLED FROM BRIDGE

Handcuff King Houdini Performs Remarkable Feat and Comes Out Safely

---

Had a Rope Tied Around His Waist and Tied To Bridge to Safeguard against Accidents

Tied by a lifeline a hundred and thirteen feet long, handcuffed with two of the best and latest model handcuffs in the possession of the Detroit police department, nerved by the confidence of a lion in his own powers...Houdini, the wonder worker at the Temple theater, leaped from the draw span of the Belle Island Bridge at 1 o'clock this afternoon, freed himself from the handcuffs while underwater, then swam to a waiting lifeboat, passed over the unlocked and open cuffs and clambered aboard.

In other words, the river was not frozen over, Houdini had a rope tied around him the whole time, he got out of only two pairs of handcuffs, and he was picked up by a boat.

Each time he told the story, he embellished it, adding to the myth of Houdini. Bess got into the act later by adding the newsboy to the story.

Coming home wasn't all about the work. During the five years he was away he had seen his mother only briefly, when she traveled to visit him in Germany. Now he spent every free moment with his beloved mother. He purchased a farm in Connecticut and a main residence in New York, a three-story brownstone in the prestigious Jewish section of Harlem. Given his never-ending touring schedule, the Harry and Bess would not see much of either house. He moved his family into the brownstone.

The show was still the straitjacket, the handcuffs, and the Metamorphosis. It was the same basic act he played the dime museums with, except now they paid him one hundred times more than his old salary of twelve dollars a week.

Ever the realist, he knew it couldn't last. He needed new novelties and plenty of them if he wanted audiences to keep showing up.

Houdini in the Milk Can (Library of Congress)

Chapter Twelve
Challenges

DURING HIS first tour of Holland, Houdini seized upon the idea of being lashed to one of the sails of a windmill and attempting to escape while it rotated. He overestimated the weight bearing strength of the sail. It broke. Houdini fell to the ground, luckily sustaining only minor scrapes and bruises.

Houdini's need for the new and novel was an unquenchable thirst. To slake it he turned to the public and challenged them to come up with a way to confine Houdini. This led to a series of sometimes bizarre, sometimes dangerous escapes.

One of his earliest was a challenge from the Wakefield Rattan Co. to escape from a large wicker hamper.

He was chained to a ladder, screwed into a zinc-lined piano case, locked in a roll-top desk, sealed in a giant paper bag, and packed in a man-sized sausage skin.

The Hogan Envelope Company of Chicago challenged Houdini to get out of the world's largest envelope.

The Pittsburg Plate Glass Company designed a specially sealed glass box.

In partnership with a sporting goods company, on January 4, 1907, the University of Pennsylvania football team sewed Houdini up in a giant football.

Nothing could hold Houdini and no one could figure out

how he accomplished these escapes.

One of Houdini's trademarks as an escape artist was that he never left any trace behind showing *the how* of his escape. The paper bag was still intact, the packing box still nailed shut, the milk can still padlocked. It was as if he had melted right through solid matter. Disturbingly, many people including his sometime friend Sir Arthur Conan Doyle believed just that: Houdini had found the secret of dematerialization.

Houdini refused such notions. He felt it was an insult. It was Houdini's skill, not supernatural foolishness, but he wasn't going to reveal his secrets just to prove them wrong.

Houdini instigated many of these challenges and then turned it around in the press to make it seem as if he was the one being challenged. When he returned to a town, a re-challenge would be set up, the "hook" being a complaint that Houdini had restricted them in some way that prevented his defeat in the first challenge. In this second challenge, this new box, bag, locks or whatever they built, free of restrictions, was sure to hold him tight.

Houdini came close to failing only twice.

On one occasion, the challenge was to escape from a large sealed vat of beer. Houdini, a teetotaler, was overcome by the alcohol and nearly drowned. He repeated the escape when he figured out that by rubbing oil on his skin he could delay the effects. (When preparing this stunt, Houdini always had the brewery send over twice as much beer as needed to fill the can, his stagehands happy to dispose of the surplus.)

The other difficult escape was also his most unusual: He escaped from a sea monster. This sentence is really just filler while that previous sentence sinks in. A sea monster. In actuality, it was a giant shell-less sea turtle that washed ashore in New England. They gutted it, preserved it, sewed Houdini up inside it, and he escaped. He very nearly passed out from the poisonous fumes of the liberally applied arsenic preservative.

Houdini always had to be on the lookout for trouble. In Chicago, he examined a pair of handcuffs offered up by an audience member, and accepted the challenge. The man cuffed Houdini's arms behind his back. He had a flashback to his early days in Chicago and Officer Waldron. He was in trouble again! The escape dragged on, but finally, he released himself. When Harry examined the handcuffs again, he realized they weren't the same cuffs. The man had switched the cuffs behind Houdini's back. A rough frisking revealed the extra pair hidden in the man's coat.

In Boston, six suffragettes wrapped Houdini up in sheets, cocoon-like, and bound him to a mattress with bandages. When sure he was fastened tight, one girl leaned over and kissed him on the cheek. Perhaps the only time he ever blushed on stage.

He improved on that escape, *NO*, not by adding more kissing, but by soaking the sheets with water. The water made the escape more difficult. He framed it as a challenge from the attendants of a lunatic asylum. He added the escape to his regular show, bringing with him his own lunatic attendants.

During one such challenge, an enthusiastic challenger pulled the sheets or straps too tight and crushed a kidney; a ruptured blood vessel began to hemorrhage. He passed blood for two weeks before he consulted a doctor. The doctor ordered rest, saying that if he continued at this pace he would be dead in a year. Houdini could not sit still very long. The kidney never healed properly and pained him for the rest of his life.

Houdini went on a buying spree, purchasing any idea he might form into a usable trick. He made one such purchase from an associate of Thomas Edison, Montraville Wood of Berwyn, Illinois. He called it the Milk Can Escape.

Constructed in Chicago, the can resembled an ordinary milk can with a flanged lid that fitted inside the neck. It stood about forty-two inches tall. The seams were riveted and soldiered watertight. Riveted to the lid of the can were six hasps, which fit over staples riveted to the neck. Six padlocks secure those hasps.

Eventually, the unthinkable happened in St. Louis: Houdini saw his name was second from the top of the bill. The manager informed him that his handcuff act didn't mean a thing at the box office and the first week's box office receipts were far below par.

Houdini knew this time would come. He had held the Milk Can Escape back for such an emergency. He opened the second week with his new blockbuster mystery.

Two assistants carried out the large galvanized-iron can to the center of the stage. An audience committee examined the container and found it remarkably unsuspicious. Houdini left the stage to change into a bathing suit while the can was filled with buckets of water.

Returning, Houdini spoke to the audience, "Ladies and gentlemen, my latest invention—The Milk Can. I will be placed in the can filled with water. The committee will lock the padlocks and place the keys down by the footlights. I will attempt to escape. Should anything happen and I should fail to appear within a certain time, my assistants will open the curtains, rush in, smash the can, and do everything possible to save my life."

74

Securely handcuffed, Houdini's assistants lifted him up and lowered him into the can feet first. It was a tight fit. He had to raise his arms above his head to squeeze down into the can. Water spilled over the sides. Extra water was added to keep the can filled to the top.

At this point, with his head just above the water, Houdini invited the audience to participate in a test. He asked them to hold their breath with him. He ducked under the water. One by one the audience gave in before Houdini came back up. He often challenged a local swimming champion to do the same. Able to hold his breath for a world record pace of three minutes, he rarely lost a contest.

After proving himself, he submerged again. When he disappeared from view, the lid was slammed on and the committee snapped the locks tight. A curtain around the can hid it from view. The orchestra played "Asleep in the Deep."

A large (the largest in the world, according to Houdini) stopwatch stood to the left of the can to count the seconds.

The audience waited. And watched.

Some of the spectators tried again to hold their breaths, but are forced to give up after a half minute or so.

One minute passes.

At ninety seconds, Houdini's trusted assistant, Franz Kukol walks to the curtain with a fire ax in his hand.

Two minutes. The audience grows restless, murmuring to each other.

Two and a half. The audience begins to clamor. Some out of their seats.

At three minutes, the audience is ready to rush the stage. Something has gone wrong!

Kukol raises the ax, ready to strike. At this moment, dripping wet, a gasping Houdini stumbles from behind the curtains. Alive!

The dull grey can sat on the stage still locked.

Houdini had a new sensational climax to the show, one that brought the audiences to their feet. It catapulted him back into the top money spots.

Houdini brought something new onto the stage. Outside, tens of thousands of people went to see his bridge jumps because of the very real element of danger. (A few copycats died trying to duplicate those jumps.) Inside the theaters, the audience saw Houdini's escapes as puzzling "tricks." With the Milk Can Escape, "failure means a drowning death" and for Houdini, that changed everything.

Houdini in Chicago ad
(*Chicago Tribune* 1926)

Chapter Thirteen
Australia

DURING THE next few years, Houdini spent his time crisscrossing the Atlantic fulfilling dates in both the old and new worlds. Bookers in Australia desperately tried to persuade Houdini to perform down under. He refused. He offered up an emotional excuse, saying his mother had not looked well and Australia was too far away if anything were to happen to her.

Circumstances would change his mind, including his stipulation that he be paid his full salary during his twelve-week boat trip. Houdini took special pleasure in "sticking it" to the bookers for those extra twelve weeks of pay. He also looked forward to a little time with Bess. He was 36 years old, but looked 50 and his hair had begun to grey.

The second circumstance was Houdini's newest passion, flight. He was racing to be the first person in Australia to fly.

In the six years since the Wright Brothers' first flight in 1903, the aviation craze had spread across the globe. Sensing the importance of air flight, aeronautic associations were formed sponsoring air meets and offering monetary prizes for distance, endurance, speed, and innovative design.

Early aviation was dangerous; between 1907 and 1910 thirty-five pilots died. In 1911, forty-one more lost their lives. It didn't matter to Houdini; it may have even helped. Aviation and Houdini were a perfect match. The public in his time, as many do today, think of Houdini as a magician. However, a closer look belies that categorization. His escapes fall more into the class of stunt than trick. In this view, Houdini is more daredevil than trickster, sharing more in common with Evel Knievel than, say, David Copperfield.

The first time he saw a plane in flight, at an air show in Paris, he envisioned being tied to its wing, escaping high in the air, and parachuting down to the spectators. Of course, that would have to wait until someone invented a way to parachute down from a plane.

In 1909, he purchased a Voisin Brothers plane for $5000. He planned to buy a Glenn Curtiss model, which had just set the speed record, but felt the Voisin looked safer. "I was but a timid bird and wanted to take no chances at the start," Houdini said.

Simple in design, the Voisin resembled the familiar biplane except for the long, square-tipped wings that were joined at the ends by vertical cloth-on-wood panels. Technically, the plane's construction was cellular. The tail consisted of one, and the wings four, rectangular boxes or cells, much like box kites, covered with sheeting used in hot air balloons. Aviators considered the Voisin a stable plane, at least in calm skies.

Houdini also imported the man who built the plane, Antonio Brassac, from France to be his mechanic and teacher. The tutoring began in Hamburg, Germany, where he was performing at the time. The government allowed him to use an army parade ground for his lessons. In exchange, he would demonstrate everything he learned about flying to the German military.

This, by the way, would be another event he would erase from his history. At the onset of World War I, Houdini destroyed all the photos of him with the German officers and shifted the story of his flying lessons to Australia.

Houdini's introduction to flying proved difficult and frustrating. Early planes were notoriously prone to mechanical problems. It was one big experiment, fixing and correcting as you went. Another problem was that early planes, especially the Voisins, were sensitive to wind. Brassac was oddly attached to this plane and would not let his baby off the ground if there were *any* wind. As a result, Houdini spent much of his time rehearsing takeoffs and landings while never leaving the ground. He could only dream of what it was like to fly.

When he finally attempted his first flight, he promptly crashed, breaking the propeller. He waited two weeks for the replacement from Paris. Then, after more bad weather, he made his first true flight. It lasted a minute and a half.

Twelve weeks later, Australia was no less troublesome. Arriving in Melbourne, it was still a twenty-mile trip to the aviation grounds at Digger's Rest. To his dismay, he found a rival there, Ralph Banks, also attempting to be the first man to fly, using a Wright Brothers built plane.

Houdini rented a forty-foot tent to house the plane and kept a grueling schedule. He spent weeks motoring to Digger's Rest after his shows and back in the afternoon to make his two-a-day performances in Melbourne. Houdini and Brassac unpacked, assembled, and tested the various parts in a blistering heat.

"Hottest day I ever lived," Houdini wrote on February 20. "Must have been 119 in the shade and the wind was scorching. Drank enough water to float a rowboat."

Because of strong winds, practices were brief or more often cancelled. When his rival Banks attempted a flight despite the wind, Houdini thought his chance was over. Brassac knew better. The Wright plane rose up thirteen or fourteen feet, suddenly swerved right, and crashed. Banks survived with a black eye and busted lips. Houdini helped clean up the wreck.

After a month of tinkering, Houdini's hopes now rested on his mechanic, Antonio Brassac. "No mother," Houdini said, "could tend her child more tenderly than Brassac does my machine."

Houdini made three flights on the morning of March 18, 1910. The first was just to test the wings. He rose up about twenty feet, flew a narrow circle, and landed. By one account, Brassac became so excited that "he forgot to speak French, and rattled off English terms of endearment to the great bird."

The second attempt went less smoothly. Houdini made a complete circle of the field covering a little over a mile. But, he forgot to straighten the elevator while landing and the plane ran along the ground for a distance on its nose. Houdini got ready to jump to safety. At the last moment, the plane righted itself.

Houdini's third flight was three and a half minutes of perfection. The plane reached an altitude of over one hundred feet and made three circuits of the field. He landed no more than twenty feet from his starting point.

The moment he hit the ground well-wishers surrounded him. Even his rival, Ralph Banks, shook his hand in congratulations. Mindful of history and his story, he had photographic record made and the spectators sign statements attesting to the feat. The magician would go on to make fourteen more flights over the next few days at Digger's Rest, including a flight that lasted more than seven minutes. Houdini was the first man to achieve flight in Australia. Still, he wasn't finished.

He had the plane shipped from Digger's Rest to Sydney so they could see him fly there as well. He rented a racetrack in Rosehill and announced "Air Week," during which he would fly daily, weather permitting. Before cheering crowds that filled the grandstand, Houdini made many successful flights. The event, so popular, was extended into May.

After one such flight, *The Daily Telegraph* reported, "men tossed up their hats; women grew hysterical and wept for sheer excitement. A hundred men rushed toward the biplane, pulled the happy aviator from his seat, and carried him, shoulder-high, mid deafening cheers and salvos."

Back in America, in August of 1911, Houdini traveled to the Midwest for the Chicago Aviation Meet held on the city's lakefront in Grant Park. Here he socialized with the elite of the aviation world, like Glenn Curtiss and Orville Wright. He sent reports back to Bess, who remained in New York for this trip:

> At one time I saw twelve machines in the air. I never before saw such wonderful sights. No accidents today. Twice I grew weak in the knees at near accidents. A Curtiss flyer, Beachy, dived 3,000 feet, but as his machine did not break, he was saved.

Houdini wrote too soon. A few days later, two pilots died in separate accidents. The day after the meet, Houdini participated in a benefit show for the flyers. His hands and feet were chained, and then he jumped from a plane that flew fifty feet above Lake Michigan, releasing himself underwater.

Houdini always intended to fly again, but he didn't. Perhaps the "timid little bird" thought this one danger too great a risk.

Houdini in flight (Library of Congress)

Chapter Fourteen
Cecilia

DURING HIS 1912 engagement at Hammerstein's in New York, Houdini made the unusual request that his entire week's salary be paid in gold pieces.

Hammerstein asked, "What's a matter? U.S. currency not good enough for you, Harry?"

"No, it's not that," Houdini said. "I got a good reason. It's personal."

With the bag of gold in hand, he rushed down to his dressing room and had two of his assistants polish up the double eagles. Once they shone, he gathered them up, took a cab up to Harlem, and went straight to his mother's room. They embraced.

"Mother, Mamma, do you remember before father died he made me promise to look after you? To take care of you, always?"

"Yes, my son."

"Well, Mother, I am now able to fulfill that promise. Hold out your apron."

He poured a shower of shimmering gold into his mother's lap. They both wept for joy.

It was the happiest moment of Houdini's life.

Houdini spent the early part of 1913 in London, but accepted a short booking in New York. It would be his only chance to see his mother that year.

The engagement was for two weeks at Hammerstein's. He laid off three more weeks, doting on his mother who, at seventy-two years old, was slowing down. Houdini was to open in Copenhagen on July 18. He waited until the last minute to sail. Beatrice remembered the departure:

Persons at the pier beheld a curious sight. They saw Houdini clinging to a little old woman in black silk, embracing and kissing her, saying goodbye and going up the gangplank only to return to embrace her again. "Ehrich, vielleicht wenn du zurück kommst bin ich nicht hier" (Perhaps when you come home I shall not be here,) his mother remarked as they reached the pier together. She was seventy-two and no longer felt any certainty about time. Houdini apparently could not leave off reassuring her and showing his affection for her. Finally she had to order him to go. Houdini, turning to the bystanders, said, "Look, my mother drives me away from her."

"No, no," protested his mother, "but you must leave now. Go quickly, and come back safe to me."

Houdini was the last person aboard. The last he saw of his mother she had caught one of the paper streamers he had thrown, and he was leaning far over the railing holding the other end.

Landing in Hamburg a week later, Houdini and Bess took the train to Copenhagen. There his assistant Franz handed him a cable from home. Busy, Houdini pocketed it. He remembered to read it the next day at a press reception. Upon reading it, he fainted and when he was brought around, he began weeping. The message said his mother was dead.

Hardeen was in America that season and was playing Asbury Park. His mother went along to see his performances. That evening, she watched Hardeen do the challenge handcuff releases, the straitjacket, and the Milk Can. Afterward, in her hotel room, Cecilia suffered a severe stroke. She died a few days later.

Houdini immediately cancelled his engagement. Arrangements were made to travel back to America, but he would be delayed several days. He cabled Hardeen and ordered him to delay the funeral. Houdini's desire to see his mother one last time took precedence over Jewish law that mandated immediate burial. Houdini's unorthodox request would not by denied by his siblings.

At the hotel Houdini was in agony. His ailing kidney flared up. The physician wanted to admit him to the hospital. He refused. The doctor accompanied Houdini on the train as far as Germany. There another doctor took over.

On July 30, Houdini stood by the grave in Machpelah Cemetery while his mother was laid to rest beside his father, Rabbi Weiss, and his half brother, Herman.

During the month of August, Houdini spent nearly every day at the grave, speaking to his mother as if she could still hear him. He was inconsolable. In the small hours of the night, Bess would hear him crying his mother's name. Later, he had the letters mother had sent him translated, typed in English, and bound in a book so he could read and reread them easily.

Over-analyzed with mostly discredited Freudian nonsense, much has been made through the years about Houdini's relationship with his mother. To put it in proper perspective, you need only look at the near canonization of motherhood in Victorian era writings. Houdini was an expression of that worship culture. Personally, he had a fiery, intense, obsessive, overemotional nature and was prone to extremes, which all contributed to his seeming over-reaction to his beloved mother's death. Besides, are Houdini's actions really any different from his father's dramatic fits after the death of his son Herman?

By September, he was able to perform again. Yet, after his first show, he had a fit of uncontrollable grief, which paralyzed him for hours.

In November from Paris, He wrote his brother, "Dash it's TOUGH, and I can't seem to get over it. Sometimes I feel alright, but when a calm moment arrives I am as bad as ever."

Time would lessen Houdini's grief but never heal it. To distract himself from his depression he threw himself into work, perfecting the ultimate illusion of cheating death, The Chinese Water Torture Cell.

Chapter Fifteen
Upside Down

"IF THE public knew how much I really flirt with death in some of my stunts, I would never be accused of getting advertising free," Houdini once told a friend.

This was never more true than with the underwater packing case escape. His first advertised escape occurred in New York, 1912 while he was playing Hammerstein's. Large banners hung at Pier A in Battery Park proclaiming, "HOUDINI will be Thrown Overboard, Nailed in a Heavy Weighted Packing Case."

Apparently New Yorkers thought this a good idea because an estimated 100,000 people showed up to see it. They lined the seawalls, filled the streets, hung out of windows, anything that could float was on the water and crammed with onlookers.

A tugboat took Houdini and a group of reporters out onto the water. The reporters examined the box and Houdini. Then Houdini was handcuffed, set in leg irons, and placed in the box. The reporters took turns nailing the lid shut. The box was weighted with two hundred pounds of iron to help it sink. Using a block and tackle, it was hoisted over the water and lowered in.

After an agonizing fifty-seven seconds, Houdini broke the surface of the water. The normally cynical New York newspapermen broke into applause and tripped over each other to help Houdini back on the boat.

The box was retrieved and inspected. It was intact. The reporters pried the lid off to find the handcuffs and irons still inside.

Due to the unique nature of the stage at Hammerstein's, which featured a 5,500-gallon water tank for aquatic acts, Houdini was able to repeat the feat nightly to tremendous response.

Each new escape—the underwater packing box, the Milk Can—was an evolutionary step forward to the Chinese Water Torture Cell. Nothing would ever top the Cell or, as Houdini called it, the Upside-Down. Unlike when he retired the Milk Can, whenever he took the Cell out of the show, he would return to it. His audiences never tired of the feat. He performed it until his death, which contrary to the movie *Houdini*, was not in the cell.

The Upside-Down combined the underwater feature and the suspense of the seconds ticking away, from the Milk Can. It added being locked in a claustrophobic cell, upside down, apparently immobilized, unable to turn around or reach up. The cell's glass front allowed the audience to see the trapped Houdini until the last moment before the curtain closed.

Houdini's team created the Upside-Down in 1911. At that time, he performed it as a two-act play for an audience of one person. This allowed Houdini to copyright the escape in England, a preemptive strike against would-be imitators. Then, he could try to sue anyone performing it. After this secret showing, he packed up the Cell and warehoused it. There it would wait for the time when audiences tired of his show or the copycat Houdinis ruined his current repertoire.

It took all of a year and a half. He premiered the Cell in Berlin at the Circus Busch, September 21, 1912.

The stage curtains opened to reveal Houdini, in evening clothes. He addressed the audience:

"Ladies and gentlemen, in introducing my original invention the Water Torture Cell, although there is nothing supernatural about it, I am willing to forfeit the sum of one thousand dollars to anyone who can prove that it is possible to obtain air inside the Torture Cell when I am locked up in the regulation manner, after it has been filled up with water."

The Cell, built in England, had cost over $10,000 dollars. A little over five and a half feet tall, it resembled a squat phone booth. The back and sides were thick mahogany in a nickel-plated steel frame. The front was half-inch tempered glass, held water tight with rubber seals.

Houdini continued, "I would like to invite eight, ten, twelve gentlemen to kindly step up on the stage. I assure you I have no confederates, and any gentleman is perfectly welcome."

Once on stage, the volunteers examined the apparatus, inspecting every part. During this procedure, Houdini went off stage and changed into a blue bathing suit. He returned wearing a robe.

Houdini offered that if any of the men thought he was using a trap door in the stage that he could move the Cell to another part. Moved or not, Houdini's assistants donned rain slickers and started, bucket by bucket, to fill the Cell with heated water.

Houdini showed the thick stocks that formed the lid of the tank. An assistant opened the jaw-like device. Houdini laid down and placed his legs in it. When closed and locked, it held his ankles fast and prevented his size seven and a half feet from slipping through.

The committee took positions surrounding the cell.

Ropes were lowered from the flies and hooked to the stocks. Hand over hand, his assistants pulled the ropes slowly raising the stocks into the air with Houdini hanging upside down from it. This was a delicate and dangerous maneuver. One sudden shift could break Houdini's ankles. This continued until Houdini was suspended over the cell.

There was a pause as Houdini drew in three deep breaths. He held the last one and clapped. Guided by two assistants he was lowered headfirst into the cell. The displaced water streamed over the sides like a broken dam.

His assistants furiously secured the stocks to the cell with padlocks. He could be clearly seen through the glass front, helpless, with his head five feet below the water, and his hands unable to reach the locks on the outside. The cabinet's curtains were drawn. The orchestra played a number. To the side, Houdini's assistant Franz Kukol stood at the ready with a fire ax.

After forty seconds, perhaps a minute, Houdini burst through the curtains, dripping wet, his eyes bloodshot, gasping for air, but he was free.

That, and only that, was what the audience had waited for. "He's done it!" "He's escaped!" "He's free!" Exclamations cried out from all parts of the audience. Then, they stood as one and applauded.

Once the audience quieted, Houdini spoke. His few words are no more than a farewell and good night. The deed spoke for itself.

"To say the applause was deafening is putting it too mildly," A London reviewer wrote. The *Stuttgart Neues Tageblatt* called it "uncommonly astonishing and awe-inspiring...A trick of incredible cunning."

Houdini was just as enthusiastic. "I believe it is the

climax of all my studies and labors. Never will I be able to construct anything that will be more dangerous or difficult for me to do."

Houdini being lowered into an early version of the
Chinese Water Torture Cell (Library of Congress)

Chapter Sixteen
Impossibilities

JUST AS Houdini's audiences were left wondering how he would next endanger himself, he set his sights in another direction. Unsatisfied with being just an escape artist, Houdini wanted to be seen in the eyes of his audience as the world's greatest magician.

During 1914 while in England, Houdini organized his *Grand Magical Review.* He eagerly filled the show with tricks plundered from magic's history. Unfortunately, Houdini's rough and tumble style was ill suited for subtle artistic presentations. All those years performing escapes had skewed his stage sensibilities. He never learned how to sell a magic effect to an audience. The show lasted no more than a dozen performances, mostly to bad reviews.

To the audiences, the name Houdini meant thrills and death-defying stunts, and they were not content to watch him perform staid magic tricks. Fine, if the audiences wanted spectacle, he'd give it to them. That spring in England, he purchased an effect that, with a few modifications, would prove to be his next astounding miracle.

The audience at Hammerstein's expected to see Houdini's newest marvel; they never expected to be watching union bricklayers build a wall. However, there they were on the stage spreading mortar and stacking the bricks, building a wall nine feet tall and ten feet wide. They worked so quickly that the audience gave them a nice hand when they finished.

Houdini invited about thirty spectators come up to examine the solid wall and the carpet-covered floor. When they were satisfied on the fair conditions, the wall, which sat on a ten-inch wide steel beam mounted on heavy casters, was rotated into place, bisecting the stage.

The committee formed a semi-circle around the back and sides of the wall leaving the front exposed to the audience.

As a jail breaker, Houdini had often been called "the man who walks through walls" and now he was going to give his audience a chance to see him do just that.

Houdini stood to one side of the structure. He couldn't go around the wall; either the audience or the committee would catch that. At nine feet tall, he could not scale it without being seen. The seamless carpet prevented him from going under via a trap door. There was only one option left: to walk through it.

Two tri-fold screens were placed against opposite sides of the wall. Houdini entered on one side. He held his hands up over the six-foot tall panels.

"Here I am," he shouted.

His hands dropped. "Now I'm going!"

"Now I'm here!" Houdini stepped from the screen on the other side of the wall.

If the members of the audience didn't think Houdini had mystical powers before, they might believe it now.

"Houdini...gave the most remarkable performance that has ever been witnessed in American vaudeville," a *Billboard* magazine reviewer wrote. "He walks through a solid brick wall without disturbing a brick. The audience sat spellbound for fully two minutes after the feat was accomplished. They were too dumbfounded to applaud."

Houdini received four curtain calls.

For such an astonishing trick, Houdini discarded it rather quickly. It was difficult to troupe from city to city. Worse, it broke his cardinal rule of secrecy. Because of the Walking Through The Wall's secret, all the stagehands, cast, and crew knew the method. It wasn't long before some unscrupulous magic dealer (a redundant term, if there ever was one) started selling plans of the trick for a dollar. Before that, he had always kept his secrets away from everyone but his most trusted assistants.

Contrary to popular myth, Houdini buried no secrets. If you are willing to do some work, read the right books, they are within your reach. Still, there was one effect that was lost for almost a hundred years and if it weren't for the detective work of one brilliant man, it may have been lost forever. It's when Houdini vanished an elephant.

There was no theater more extreme than the Hippodrome in New York City. Opened in 1905, it filled the full 6th Avenue block between 43rd and 44th Streets. The theater sat 5,200. The stage was near the size of a football field and could hold six hundred performers.

The theater held grand shows of spectacular tableaus and oversized vaudeville including marching choruses of soldiers, Power's dancing elephants, high-diving horses, and huge reproductions of entire city blocks. The stage looked positively empty if there weren't at least a hundred people on it. There was only one man with the audacity and bravado to fill the stage alone. That was Houdini.

He joined their show *Cheer Up* in January 1918. He bragged he would perform the smallest and the largest illusions in magic. He opened with the smallest, his dependable Needles.

To fill the stage, he used an improbable two hundred needles and sixty feet of thread. Except for a faint shimmer as they caught the spotlight, the needles could not be seen much beyond the first couple of rows. Houdini's showmanship brought the trick over. Friend and fellow magician, The Great Leon, summed it up when he said, "They knew there were needles because Houdini told them so."

What happened next is not so clear. Although an estimated one million people saw the illusion during his nineteen week run at the Hippodrome, there are few good accounts of the elephant vanishing. An overly enthusiastic Houdini told it his way in a letter to *Sphinx* magazine (a trade magazine for magicians) publisher, Dr. A. M. Wilson.

I have been prolonged at the Hippodrome as the vanishing elephant has created so much talk, and really it is the biggest vanish the world has ever seen.

I have a wonderful elephant, and it is stated she is the daughter of the famous Barnum Jumbo.

I use a cabinet about eight foot square, about twenty-six inches off the floor, it is rolled on by twelve men. [Houdini left out the depth of about fifteen feet.] I show all parts, opening the back and front. The elephant walks into it, I close the doors and curtains. (Doors in the back and curtains in the front), and in two seconds I open back and front and she is gone. No special background, in full glare of the light, and it is a weird trick. In

96

fact, everyone says, "We don't see enough of it." They are so busy watching for a false move that, though the trick takes seven or eight minutes, it appears like a few seconds.

The elephant salutes me, says goodbye to the audience by waving her trunk and head, turns to me, lifts up her trunk as if to give me a kiss; in fact, I say to the audience, "Jennie will now give me a kiss," but she is really coming to me with her mouth open for sugar, with which I trained her. I introduce her as the first known Vanishing Elephant.

She has a baby blue ribbon around her neck, and a fake wristwatch on her left hind leg, so the audience can see her leg until the last second, when she enters the cabinet. I say, "She is all dressed up like a bride," and that gets a big laugh; for the good-natured beast lumbers along, and I believe she is the best natured elephant that ever lived. I never allowed a hook to be used, relying on block sugar to make her go through her stunt, and she is certainly fond of me.

She weighs over ten thousand pounds, and as gentle as a kitten.

Everything is in bright light. It is no black art, and it is a wonderful mystery.

The Hippodrome billed it as "The Most Colossal Disappearing Mystery that History Records." But most of the audience was disappointed. A magician's magazine noted:

The Hippodrome being of such a colossal size, only those sitting directly in front got the real benefit of the deception. The few hundred people sitting around me took Houdini's word for it that the "animile" had gone—we couldn't see into the cabinet at all!

Despite the disappointment, Houdini knew the value in the illusion was in the publicity. Millions of people, unable to go to the Hippodrome, would read that Houdini was the man who made an elephant disappear. It was the illusion that earned him the reputation he sought, Magician.

Aside from that, no one could explain how the damned thing worked. Magicians tried to dismiss it with a joke by saying, the cabinet took three men to wheel out and twenty men to push it off stage. Of course, it was not true. Houdini was too careful a magician to make such a foolish mistake. The joke tells more about what the magicians' thought of Houdini's abilities and their jealousy over his fame.

Their dismissal of the trick's secret showed how badly the magicians were fooled. It may have been a great trick disguised as a bad trick by Hippodrome's poor staging and Houdini's simple presentation. It didn't matter; by ignoring the illusion, the secret was lost. Eighty years later, one of magic's brightest minds, Jim Steinmeyer discovered it after years of dogged detective work. He pieced together small fragments of evidence that littered history and teased out the solution.

Are you curious? Great!

That is Jim's story to tell and it's not my place to tell it. Jim wrote an amazing book about his quest. If you want to know how Houdini vanished the elephant (and a cool look into the secret world of magicians) read his wonderful book, *Hiding the Elephant, How Magicians Invented the Impossible and Learned to Disappear.*

Houdini's new sensations made headlines, increased his fame, and ballooned his salary by thousands of dollars a week. They also served another purpose. They saved his body from the rigors of the escapes. The years had piled up. Houdini was in near constant pain. If he was going to continue to perform on stage, magic had to succeed. But the difficulty in traveling with these impossibilities forced him to search for a new sensation. When, he found it, he made it a great moral crusade.

Houdini and Jennie (Library of Congress)

Chapter Seventeen
Spiritualism

IT WAS 1848, the world of Edgar Allan Poe, all shadows and gaslights and candles, and parlors with heavy velvet draperies. With disease, poor medical practices, often-dangerous living conditions, death gleefully stalked the world. A world waking up to the possibilities of science, but still clinging to their superstitions and religions.

In 1848, modern spiritualism was born. Spiritualism is the belief that the consciousness survives after death. One large component of this belief is that communication with the dead is possible. It turned into something of a craze, a fad. People from all walks of life attended séances, including presidents and queens. Séances became the popular entertainment of the time. Some reacted with thunderous outrage; the very idea of talking to the dead must be sorcery or devil worship. Others saw it as confirmation of their religious belief of life after death.

Modern spiritualism began in America in Hydesville, New York, with the Fox sisters, Margaret and Kate, both young children at the time. Almost as soon as the Fox family moved into their small rustic cottage, the rapping noises began, a sound not unlike knuckles knocking on the floor or wall. Mr. Fox investigated, but he could find no natural explanation for the strange noises. Some neighbors insisted the house had always been haunted.

Then on March 31, 1848, something amazing happened. Mrs. Fox and her young daughter, Kate, were alone in the house when the rapping noises began.

Little Kate looked up into the empty space and said, "Here Mr. Splitfoot, do as I do."

She snapped her fingers three times. Almost immediately, three raps sounded.

Kate then reached up and made the motion of snapping her fingers twice, but without making a sound.

Two raps replied.

"Mother," she said, "it can see as well as hear."

The news of the communication spread like a rash that needed to be scratched. The townspeople besieged the little cottage, all desperate for a message from beyond. It wasn't just happening in New York; suddenly, people all over America were miraculously discovering they, too, had the power to communicate with the dead.

In the next few years, the Fox sisters would become the most famous spirit mediums of their day. They conducted thousands of séances. Then, in 1888, forty years after the event, Margaret Fox confessed she never believed in spirits, that spiritualism was a fraud of the worse deception, and the rapping noises were made by the cracking of the joints of her toes. She demonstrated the feat to a rapt audience at the New York Academy of Music in New York.

Even though the Fox sisters had confessed, they inspired thousands of other spiritualist mediums in the 19th Century. All of whom insisted that, unlike the women they copied, they themselves were genuine.

Those who copied the Fox Sisters improved on them as well. The sisters could only receive simple messages, by a process of reciting the alphabet and waiting for a rap on the appropriate letter, then repeating that laborious process over and over until they spelled an entire word. Other mediums developed the more expedient technique of using small pieces of chalkboard, actually children's school slates, for spirits to write messages on.

"Voice mediums" used a long tin cone or spirit trumpet to allow the spirits to talk to the sitters, others just, to use a modern word, channeled the spirits and let them use their own vocal chords to speak through.

There were physical mediumships where the mediums produced apparitions of hands, faces and the full bodies of the departed.

All of this happened in complete darkness because the spirits could only work in the dark. Yet, when they appeared, the spirits had this remarkable glow about them, as if someone held them under a bright light for a while.

The shooting star that was spiritualism burned brightest during the years right after that first communication and lasted until after the Civil War. It faded in the late 1800s, resurging again in the 1920s after WWI.

As we know, Houdini and his wife performed séances, so they knew the racket from the inside. Through the years, he had kept an observer's interest in spirit mediums, knowing their secret techniques and masterful psychology would be useful to a magician. He even met with some former mediums. One of the earliest and most famous, Ira Davenport of the Davenport Brothers revealed his secrets to Houdini.

The Davenports used a small cabinet to provide the privacy the spirits needed to appear. The brothers' act consisted of them being tied securely with rope inside the cabinet. Secretly, they escaped the ropes and produced the ghostly manifestations. It was a direct forerunner of Houdini's escape act.

When Houdini met Sir Arthur Conan Doyle in 1920, he was pushed into the fight over spiritualism. It is no surprise Houdini sought friendship with Doyle, the artist-intellectual-man of letters. He was the respectable man Houdini wanted to be. However, the Doyle Houdini met was not the man he expected, a man of science and logic like Sherlock Holmes. Instead, Sir Arthur Conan Doyle was an embarrassing standard-bearer for credulity.

Doyle believed in all sorts of nonsense and denied all evidence to the contrary. He wrote a book promoting the preposterous Cottingley Fairies photographs as reality. (If he had done a little detective work, he would have found that the fairies were cut out of a popular children's book published in 1915, a book that featured one of his own stories.) When a medium was caught in a deception, Doyle excused it as something the mediums resorted to when their powers were low and they still wanted to satisfy their audience. Most frustrating to Houdini, Doyle refused to believe that Houdini performed his tricks by skill.

Houdini once performed for Doyle a simple beginner's magic stunt where it appeared that he removed his thumb. It was a childish thing really. Doyle took it for real. Houdini tried explaining that nothing supernatural was involved with anything he did. Doyle just became more convinced Houdini was hiding his real occult powers.

"I heard of your remarkable feat in Bristol," Doyle wrote to Houdini after he escaped from a packing case. "My dear chap, why go around the world seeking a demonstration of the occult when you are giving one all the time?"

Houdini played coy about his intentions regarding the

spirit mediums with Doyle. He wanted to visit mediums to collect information on their techniques, but he was finding it difficult. The mediums feared Houdini was there to make trouble. With an introduction from Doyle, Houdini visited hundreds of noted spiritualists.

Houdini's diary reflects his disappointment. "I went to 100 spiritualistic séances trying to discover something new—it is the same routine," and "All this is ridiculous stuff."

Friends pressured Houdini to expose the mediums' racket. He still wanted to wait. He needed access and that would be lost once he exposed their tricks. Even now, he was forced to use confederates, who were also magicians, to go to séances in his place and act as informants. In addition, he believed, or at least he wanted to believe.

He supported the basic tenet of spiritualism that consciousness survives after death. He hoped to find someone could actually speak to the dead. All he found was an elaborate confidence game played under a mask of piety.

The beginning of Houdini's crusade and the end of the friendship between Doyle and Houdini is traced to one event, the day Doyle's wife contacted the spirit of Houdini's dear mother.

Houdini learning the tricks of the trade from reformed
Chicago medium Annie Benninghofen in 1926
(Library of Congress)

Chapter Eighteen
Séances

DURING 1922, Conan Doyle was on the America lecture circuit to preach the gospel of spiritualism. While visiting Atlantic City with his family, he invited Harry and Bess to join them at the ocean for a weekend of relaxation. Houdini, who loved children and always regretted that he and Bess could have none, swam with Sir Arthur's children and taught them how to dive and float. Between lessons, Doyle worked to convert Houdini to spiritualism.

They discussed spirit photography. Arthur showed great enthusiasm for the "extras" or ghosts that appeared in the photographs. Houdini stayed mum. He was suspicious of the photographs. He had recently taken up a study of photography and tricked up a number of spirit photographs himself.

Doyle told Houdini about the wonderful mind readers he met in Washington, the Zancigs. He described to Houdini their demonstrations in telepathy and how they could not possibly be performed with trickery. What wonderful gifts they possessed! Again, Houdini kept quiet, but he must have fumed. Houdini had worked with The Zancigs on the vaudeville stage and they were members of the Society of American Magicians. Any evidence to the contrary would be ignored by Doyle anyway.

Doyle would be no better a judge of Houdini's state of

mind than the veracity of the mediums he sat sucker for. On Sunday, he asked Houdini for a private meeting. Lady Doyle, who practiced automatic writing, wanted to give him a special séance. She had a strong feeling that a message might come through.

The curtains were drawn. On the table was a tablet of writing paper and two pencils. To one side of Lady Doyle sat her husband; on the other, Houdini.

Doyle bowed his head, said a little prayer, and called for "another sign from our friends from beyond." He reached out and touched his wife's hands.

Suddenly, she convulsed and seized a pencil. She appeared to resist, but finally gave in and let the pencil write.

She drew a cross at the top of the pad.

Then she filled up the pad with scribblings, page after page. Arthur tore the pages away and handed the sheets to Houdini.

He read, "Oh, my darling, thank God, thank God, at last I'm through—I've tried, oh so often—now I am happy. Why, of course, I want to talk to my boy—my own beloved boy..." The tripe went on for fifteen pages.

Houdini and Doyle wrote vastly differing and ever-changing accounts of the séance, but even Doyle admitted that Houdini looked "grimmer and paler" as he read the message from his "mother."

Too polite to admonish his friends, Houdini kept silent, but he would not stay that way much longer. Houdini found much about that day to feel wrong about.

Bess had already tipped Houdini that the previous night Lady Doyle had pumped her for information on Houdini's mother and their relationship. No wonder Lady Doyle felt that a message might come through.

The cross at the top of the letter was a suspicious way for his mother, the wife of a rabbi, to confirm her fidelity to God.

The sappy words were difficult to swallow since, it didn't sound like his mother. Her English was equally surprising, since he said his mother never learned English.

Even more disturbing, the day of the séance, coincidentally, was Cecilia's birthday, and she never mentioned it in the course of dictating fifteen pages.

Four months later Houdini would seal the fate of the relationship when he wrote an article entitled "Spirit Compacts Unfilled." One sentence, that Houdini wrote, in particular enraged Lady Doyle. "My mind is open. I am perfectly willing to believe, but in twenty-five years of my investigation and hundreds of séances, which I have attended, I have never seen or heard anything that could convince me that there is a possibility of communication with loved ones who have gone beyond."

Besides being an affront to Lady Doyle, the comments embarrassed Sir Arthur who had been spreading the word that Houdini was a convert. Houdini couldn't play nice any more. He had to attack.

From being a part-time student of Spiritualism, Houdini rapidly became an internationally recognized authority and aggressive investigator. His disgust over the moral implications of mediumship, his desire to be seen as more than a magician, and his keen observations that Doyle's lecture played to full houses, all combined to set Houdini on a path to give anti-spiritualistic lectures.

The lecture ran up to two hours depending on the audience. Houdini presented himself as a seeker of truth. He told stories of his own time as a medium and his turning against such things. He showed glass slides of important moments in the history of spiritualism. He demonstrated the "how to" of séance frauds.

He also tested would-be miracle men like a Spanish psychic named Argamasilla, who claimed to see through metal. Houdini easily figured out the method. Afterward, *Billboard* magazine wrote, "Battling Houdini went up against the Spanish kid...and knocked the X out of the latter's X-ray eye."

In the spring of 1924, Houdini finally published a book length exposé on spiritualism, *A Magician Among The Spirits.* The book got favorable reviews. The press bestowed Houdini with the mantle of public benefactor.

Houdini was privately disappointed in the final product. The publisher had cut out over 100,000 words. The remaining text had been revised to the point it was almost unrecognizable. Yet, it still is an entertaining look into the séance room and Houdini's passionate warnings could easily apply to today's millions who are hoodwinked by channelers, transcendentalists, gurus, faith healers, new age hucksters, homeopaths, and assorted television psychics.

In addition to open tests, Houdini often would put on his old handcuff king buster disguise to attend séances secretly. He tracked down George Rennan, a voice medium, who could produce ghost voices from a spirit trumpet for a dollar a ghost. While examining the tin trumpet Houdini smudged some lampblack on the mouthpiece. When the lights came up, the medium had black rings around his mouth.

When a young medium named Nino Pecoraro had almost convinced the magazine *Scientific American* that he was for real, Houdini cancelled his engagements and ran to the rescue. Despite being tied up with rope, Nino was still able to ring bells and jangle tambourines. It was the old Davenport Brothers trick. Houdini knew that using the 75-foot length of rope to tie Nino would not work. It is too easy to get enough slack to escape. Houdini bound Nino with short pieces of fishing line. All that Nino was able to produce in that séance were curses towards Houdini.

Mina Crandon, known as Margery, would be Houdini's hardest test for *Scientific American*. The odds were stacked against him proving her a fraud. Several of the other investigators struck up a more than cozy relationship with the married medium. One even moved in with her and her husband. Houdini, the prim Victorian, was up to the task. He discovered her fraud. When she found out that he would reveal her deception she first begged him to stop.

"How would it look for my twelve year old son to grow up and read that his mother was a fraud?"

"Then don't be a fraud," Houdini suggested.

When that didn't work, she threatened violence. Her husband tried to bribe Houdini. He didn't bite. Instead, he published a book exposing Margery and demonstrated her fraud on stage.

Houdini's lectures were effecting the spiritualism business. After he left Los Angeles, the police raided the National Spiritualist Association and indicted ten of its top officers on conspiracy and fraud.

In Chicago, 1,500 spiritualists met to protest Houdini's attacks on their religion. Houdini estimated he was being sued for over one million dollars by the mediums he exposed.

In a séance, Margery announced that Houdini had "but one more year to live."

Houdini knew from the experiences of his old friend, Joe Rinn, a skilled debunker himself, that the spiritualists were

ruthless in dealing with their antagonists.
Houdini started carrying a derringer.

Houdini with his mother, Cecilia and wife, Bess
(Library of Congress)

Chapter Nineteen
Spook Busting

HOUDINI CHALLENGED the spiritualists with a $10,000 prize to any who could fool him. Rather than waiting for the spirit mediums to show up, Houdini took the fight to them. He hired a team of investigators to infiltrate their séance rooms. His private operatives snuck into town days ahead of Houdini's scheduled appearances. They would attend séances and report the goings on to Houdini.

He recruited mostly female investigators—actresses, showgirls, even his niece. They posed as small town widows, jealous wives, naïve store clerks, and neurotic schoolteachers. The mediums saw the easy prey and dreamed of fat wallets. His chief investigator, Rose Mackenberg, investigated, by her own estimate, over three hundred mediums. For as little as five dollars, she was ordained repeatedly as a full-fledged spiritualistic reverend, all under the name Frances Raud. F.RAUD.

"To be a real minister you have to spend eight to eighteen years," Houdini told his audiences, "but to be a spiritualist minister you just have to say, 'I hear voices.'"

The spiritualist exposé was one part, the climax, of Houdini's biggest show ever. By 1925, vaudeville's death rattle could be heard. The motion pictures were beginning their reign as the dominate choice for entertainment. Houdini left vaudeville and for the 1925-1926 season, he toured with a full evening show.

Building on the press notices he received from his lectures, Houdini launched a publicity rocket that exploded in every city he appeared. While his agents fed him information on local mediums, he was disclosing their findings to the press. The headlines fueled the public, eager to see him expose the charlatans in person.

Writers, present company included, revel over the screaming headlines extolling Houdini's exploits, but it wasn't that easy, even for Houdini, to make the front pages. Checking the archives of a newspaper like the *Chicago Tribune,* make it seem as if Houdini was a mere footnote at the same time he was front-page news in the *Chicago American.*

It was Houdini's specialty to work a deal to plant stories or give that newspaper an exclusive to get the preferred space. Houdini called the exploitation of his headline getting stunts "circusing up," after the lessons in promotion he learned from his days in the circus. Houdini's campaign peaked in Chicago during an incredible eight-week springtime run at the Princess Theatre.

In contrast to his thirty-minute vaudeville turns, the new show ran two and a half hours but because of the free-for-all nature of the spiritualism exposé segment it often ran over three hours. The show was divided into three acts with two ten-minute intermissions.

In the first act, *Magic,* Houdini performed some fifteen ever-changing large-scale tricks and illusions. The curtains opened to a stage set with tables and magical apparatus. A clock chimed. Houdini entered in full evening clothes, bowed, and then startlingly ripped off his sleeves. He performed this first part of the show in an odd short-sleeved coat. It was a historical nod to the magician Bosco (1793-1863) who performed in a similar styled coat in his show. It proved the old adage, "nothing up the sleeves."

Houdini's first effect was another tribute, this time to Robert-Houdin and his Crystal Casket. A small glass box was isolated and hung in the air from two delicate chains. By sleight of hand, Houdini vanished several silver dollars. With a wave of an empty hand, the coins reappeared inside the glass box with a loud "CLINK."

The trip through the history of magic continued with Dr. Lynn's Palingenesia, where a man appears to have his arms, legs, and head cut off in succession and then, restored to his pre-dismembered condition. The program noted the effect "startled and pleased your Grand and Great-Grand Parents."

In the course of the next hour, Houdini vanished and produced quantities of clocks, silks, fishbowls, coins (again, but in a different trick), cards, flowers, and scantily clad flappers. In addition, he was always ready in case something went wrong and he needed to perform the Needles.

The newspapers mostly gave Houdini's magic excellent reviews. The *Chicago Tribune* reviewer said, "Houdini gives a bang up entertainment, knows the trick of investing the informal proceedings with opportune drama, and deserves attention for his skill as a necromancer."

From his peers, the reaction was mixed. The editor of *The Sphinx* thought it surpassed anything since Kellar. (In his time, everyone ranked Kellar as the greatest magician in America and he was one of the few living magicians Houdini admired.) On the other hand, a reviewer in *The Sphinx* wrote, "rather a disappointment—too long, too unpolished, and too much The Great Houdini: the word 'I'...is overworked all through."

Houdini called the second act, *Houdini Himself, In Person*. This act was a "greatest hits" selection of his escapes. Like the *Magic* act, the escapes varied. He started out the run performing the straitjacket, the Metamorphosis (the first time Bess had performed in years), and the Water Torture Cell. In longer runs, he added challenges like the packing cases and the wet sheets.

If his magic polarized magicians, his escapes did not. This was the Houdini no one could top.

Everything until now led to Act Three: *Do the Dead Come Back?* By now, Houdini had refined this part of his show into an entertaining romp through a gallery of spiritualistic rogues and their underhanded methods.

He began, "I have all the reason to believe this is the most important part of the evening's entertainment and long after you have forgotten everything that has gone on before. I feel certain you will not forget some of the things said and done in the next thirty or forty-five minutes."

He spoke earnestly and passionately like a born-again tent show preacher. He reminded the audience of his $10,000 challenge. He gloated over his past exposures and threatened to expose every one of Chicago's three hundred mediums. He told of the $1,000,000 worth of lawsuits brought against him by angry spiritualists. Do not fear, nothing would silence Houdini.

The audiences ate it up. Houdini named Chicago mediums from the stage, many of whom were in the audience, too curious to stay away from the show. He would literally turn the spotlight on them and tell the audience of the fraud that went on in their séance rooms and fortune telling parlors.

116

He told stories of how the mediums materialized husbands that never existed and got messages from children who were never born. When they yelled back that it was a lie, his investigators stood up and testified to the accuracy of the information. Dramatically, his lady investigators faced the audience in black, like mourning widows, with dark veils covering their faces to preserve their anonymity.

In Chicago alone, his investigators exposed seventy-nine fraud mediums. The *Chicago American* joined with Houdini to corner Mrs. Minnie Reichert during a basement séance. In attendance were nineteen sitters, eight in league with the magician. With the lights out, Minnie produced voices from her spirit trumpet. A flash bulb went off. In the chaos that followed, the camera was passed hand to hand among Houdini's crew, five of whom squeezed out the basement window. The photo filled the front page and showed Minnie raising the trumpet to her lips with a handkerchief to avoid leaving fingerprints.

Houdini pulled no punches. In Philadelphia, he agreed to debate a group of spiritualists on whether the Bible supported the validity of their mediumships. After the representatives of the Spiritual Union sat on the stage, Houdini opened with a devastating blow.

Witness to the event, author Walter B. Gibson later wrote, "Facing the packed audience, Houdini made a sweeping sidearm gesture toward the seated group onstage; he announced: 'Ladies and gentlemen, seated before you is the largest aggregation of ruthless swindlers and outright frauds ever assembled at one time in the city of Philadelphia.'"

There was a moment of stunned silence before the spiritualist sympathizers started screaming only to be drowned out by the jeers and catcalls from Houdini's supporters. A near riot ensued. After control was established, the debate continued with Houdini the ultimate victor.

This happened, in some form, in every city he visited. The fighter in Houdini loved it. Forget reality television. This was reality.

Houdini didn't stop at talk. He brought volunteers onstage so he could recreate a sham séance. In a novel idea, since he couldn't turn down the lights, he fitted his audience assistants with black hoods to simulate the darkness of the séance room.

He proceeded to replicate the tricks of the mediums. He showed how he could free one hand while the volunteers thought they were holding both. He released his foot to ring a bell with his toes. He switched blank slates for ones with spirit messages. The theater audience laughing and whooping it up as they saw the secrets and the blinded onstage volunteers were left befuddled.

Professionally and artistically, the tour was a triumph. "I have been told," Houdini said, "this is the biggest hit ever made by any magician." At fifty-two years old, he was at the peak of his career.

Chapter Twenty
Superman

THE 1925-1926 season ended in May after Houdini
testified in front of Congress in favor of an anti-fortune telling
bill. The bill did not pass, but Houdini's raucous antics at the
hearings put the magician on the front pages again.

Now that he had four months off, Houdini said he'd rest.
Instead, he continued his investigations of the spiritualists,
including delving deep into their backgrounds. He amassed
thousands of pages of information.

He reviewed the increasing number of lawsuits and even
sold off some assets to pay his legal fees.

He worked with his ghostwriters, one of whom was the
legendary horror writer, H. P. Lovecraft, on a
comprehensive book about superstitions.

As Houdini pushed himself physically and mentally, his
sleep patterns became more erratic. He normally slept five or
six hours a night, but now he was up at all hours. His
behavior was also affected. He demanded his friends to come
over in the middle of the night for something important, and
upon arriving, they would find the emergency was to see the
newest acquisition for his book collection.

He showed increasing signs of paranoia and in some of
his late night phone calls, ranted about how the spiritualists
were going to kill him.

There were reports of violent and aggressive

confrontations. Because a Los Angeles newspaper failed to publish a picture of him, he charged into the pressroom and "raised hell." When he learned of the Houdina Radio Company in New York, he lost all reason. Convinced they were exploiting his name, he confronted the owners. He took a chair and busted the electric chandelier then started destroying the other furniture. The Houdina Company, it turned out, was actually owned by a family named Houdina.

A different kind of fraud spurred Houdini to attempt a draining test of physical endurance.

An Egyptian fake, Rahman Bey, claimed his supernatural powers allowed him to control his pulse, pierce his cheeks with hatpins without bleeding, and cheat death by being buried alive in an airtight coffin. Bey performed the stunt by remaining in the coffin for one hour while submerged in a pool.

Houdini seethed. He already exposed this sideshow nonsense in his book, *Miracle Mongers and Their Methods.* He wrote in the *Evening World,* "I guarantee to remain in any coffin that the fakir (fuh-keer) does for the same length of time he does, without going into any cataleptic trance."

Houdini trained his body for three weeks, progressively testing his endurance in an airtight coffin.

On August 5, 1926, Houdini entered the Hotel Shelton ready for his challenge. The Boyertown Burial Casket Company furnished the coffin. It was a plain box of galvanized iron, six and a half feet long, two feet wide, and two feet tall. Some physicians estimated the air would only last four or five minutes. They were off by ninety minutes. The stunt took a lot out of Harry. When released from the coffin, he ran with perspiration and was deathly pale. That evening he felt weak and listless.

Experiencing physical and mental exhaustion, Houdini began his fall tour on September 7, 1926 in Boston. It was fraught with problems. He hired a court stenographer to sit on stage and record everything said during his spiritualism exposé to help fight the lawsuits.

In Providence, he lost more sleep, staying up all night to tend to Bess when she became ill with food poisoning. He only snatched a few hours sleep over the next several days as her illness lingered.

In his next stop, Albany, just as Houdini was hoisted up for the Water Torture Cell, the cables jerked. Houdini grimaced in pain and signaled to be lowered. A doctor came out of the audience and examined Houdini in the wings. He thought Houdini should go to the hospital at once; his ankle was broken.

Houdini waved him off. He wouldn't disappoint his fans. Unable to stand on one leg, he hopped out on one foot and continued the show by performing the Needle trick. After the intermission, he gave his Act Three anti-spiritualist demonstration from a chair. Only after the show did he go to the hospital.

Now more than ever he believed his own superhuman publicity. With the help of his mechanics, overnight they fashioned a brace for his leg and he never missed a performance.

On Tuesday October 19, he was in Montreal to give an anti-spiritualist speech to the students at McGill University. He began by explaining some of the rudiments of magic, so the students might understand the natural means of deception. He lauded the religion of Spiritualism, but showed contempt for the "religious racketeers" who preyed on the most vulnerable people. Later, the attendees said they thought he looked drawn and worn.

What happened over the next couple of days was pieced together from sketchy witness statements and conflicting memories. On Thursday October 21, Houdini hosted a few students, one an artist, Sam Smiley, in his dressing room. Smiley was to draw a portrait of him. His ankle still a severe problem, Houdini reclined on a couch, going through his mail as the artist drew.

Later J. Gordon Whitehead, a McGill theology student, joined them. He was there to return a book he had borrowed from Houdini. In the course of the conversation, he pressed Houdini about some rumors that he could take a punch without injury. Houdini tried to steer away from a confrontation. Hovering over Houdini, Whitehead persisted.

As he began to get up off the sofa, Whitehead punched Houdini hard, four or five times, low, just to the right of his navel. The other students pulled Whitehead off. He attacked Houdini.

Houdini winced and mumbled, "That will do."

Smiley quickly finished the portrait. Houdini seemed pleased and asked him to sign it. "You made me look a little tired in this picture," Houdini said. "The truth is I don't feel so well."

He admitted to still being in pain at dinner that night.

He made it through the Friday evening performance, complaining about the pain. He got little sleep that night because he started cramping as well. Bess rubbed his stomach with some alcohol.

Exhausted from the restless night, he almost fell asleep during the Saturday matinee. He complained of awful pain in his stomach to his wife's nurse. She gave him some medicine for indigestion.

During the evening show intermissions, he retired to his dressing room couch, in a cold sweat. After the show, he was too weak to dress himself in his street clothes. He refused to see a doctor. He was scheduled to appear in Detroit the next night. He had to catch the train, but his pain got so severe, they wired ahead for a doctor to meet them. Houdini arrived in Detroit with a fever of 102. The doctor thought it was an attack of appendicitis. Houdini was determined to give the opening night performance. He was Houdini after all.

At curtain, his temperature had risen to 104. He stumbled through the magic weak and distracted. When he left the stage, he collapsed, but after the intermission, he willed himself back onstage. Somehow, he finished the show.

He still refused to go to the hospital until several hours later and after consultations with the house physician, with Dr. Kennedy the chief of surgery at Grace Hospital, and a phone call to his own doctor in New York. Dr. Kennedy operated on Houdini at three in the afternoon, October 25.

When Dr. Kennedy made the first exploratory incision, puss flowed from Houdini's abdomen onto the floor. His appendix had ruptured, allowing deadly poison to seep into his system. The doctor removed the infected organ.

Privately, the doctors gave Houdini twelve hours to live. Like most of the predictions ever made about Houdini, they were wrong. By Tuesday, he had improved. His temperature dropped. His appetite returned.

On Friday October 29, peritonitis had developed, and the poison had spread to his intestines, paralyzing them. A second operation was ordered. Houdini reacted well to it. He remained conscious and aware, sharing stories of his life with the doctors. On Saturday, he composed a letter to a friend.

Sometime during the night, Houdini took a turn for the worse. By the early afternoon, the doctors knew it would end soon. Houdini's brothers Nathan and Hardeen sat with him. Harry looked to Hardeen and said, "I guess I'm all through fighting."

On Sunday October 31, 1926 at 1:26 P.M., Houdini drew his last breath.

Houdini portrait (Library of Congress)

Chapter Twenty-one
Endings

EVEN AFTER his death Houdini was in control. He left specific instructions on how his funeral and internment was to be carried out. The funeral was held on November 4 at the Elk's Lodge on West Forty-Third Street in New York. Over two thousand people filled the ballroom. Thousands more crowded the streets outside.

The magicians' fraternity he founded, The Society of American Magicians, wrote a special funeral rite for the occasion, a rite performed at the funerals of members to this day.

He was buried next to his mother in Machpelah Cemetery with his head resting on a pillow stuffed with the letters she had written to him.

The New York World wrote, "Starting out as a magician, he developed so much that by the end of his career he had fairly earned the title scientist."

The New York Times noted he was "a man of wide reading, a collector both of books and art."

The New York Sun grieved, "His death removes a great artist and useful scientist, and he was both without impairment of the qualities of heart and soul that endeared him to his fellows of the stage and his unnumbered admirers in front of the footlights."

"Houdini was one of the great showmen by far," wrote

the humorist Will Rogers. "Now he had that something that no one can define that is generally just passed off under the heading of showmanship. But it was in reality, Sense, Shrewdness, Judgment, unmatched ability, Intuition, Personality, and an uncanny knowledge of people."

His friend and fellow magician, Charles Carter, summed up Houdini in these words: "He was much maligned and generally misunderstood. His life was unselfish and devoted always to the betterment of those he loved and those less fortunate. His deeds of charity were manifold. So unostentatious was he in such acts that only his closest friends were cognizant of them."

A few days later, at a memorial service, the movie star Eddie Cantor broke down and had to be helped off the stage in the midst of eulogizing his friend.

Bess executed Houdini's will. His collection of over five thousand rare magic books went to the Library of Congress. She gave some of his magic collection to friends. The drama books and much of his prized collection of ephemera was sold. What she couldn't sell, the junk man hauled away. It was, reportedly, wagon loads of keys, locks, and handcuffs. What she couldn't sell or junk, she threw in the trash heap including hundreds of Houdini's letters that now sell for $1000 to $1500 each. She sold the Brownstone, moved to a smaller house, and spent her days living off the invested interest.

What do you do when your whole life is lived in the service of one man's all consuming will and that purpose is taken away? For Bess, it meant she would drift. For years, Harry hid her drinking. But without Harry, her alcoholism became more pronounced. Always a free spirit, she fell prey to young gigolos. Things became so bad, Hardeen stepped in to gain some control over her finances before it was all gone.

In 1934, Bess moved to Los Angeles where she met Edward Saint. He lived up to his name. He was a magician, carnival outside talker, crystal gazer. Saint controlled Beatrice's drinking, managed her career as the wife of Houdini, and worked full time to keep the memory of Houdini alive. His most effective publicity stunts were the Houdini séances he hosted for ten years.

Each year on October 31, the anniversary of Houdini's death, Saint would gather a group of Houdini's friends and plead for Houdini to return from beyond with a message.

Hardeen inherited Houdini's magic and continued performing. He never reached anywhere near the heights of his brother's fame, but he lived a comfortable life working dates in remnants of the vaudeville circuits. He spent five years on Broadway in Olsen and Johnson's *Hellsapoppin.* He performed all of Houdini's tricks, except one, the Upside-Down. The tank was much too small for the taller Hardeen.

Edward Saint died at fifty-one years old in 1942, and out of Bess's life went the only peace and happiness she had known since Houdini left her. She lived in a nursing home for a time. She was determined to go back home, but on the train from Los Angeles to New York, she died. It was February 11, 1943.

Before her death, Bess told friends that if a medium ever announced a message from her it would be a fraud. "When I go, I'll be gone for good. I won't even try to come back."

Her niece Marie Hinson claimed that at the end Bess had

re-embraced the Catholic religion. Her family disobeyed her wishes to be buried alongside Houdini. She was laid to rest in a Catholic cemetery in Westchester.

Hardeen had started to write a book about his brother when went into the hospital for an operation. He never came out. He died on June 12, 1945.

Doctors continue to debate if J. Gordon Whitehead's punch could have caused Houdini's ruptured appendix. The public made their decision. Whitehead lived out his days as a virtual recluse, opting for obscurity rather than infamy as "the man who killed Houdini." He died in 1954.

Every year dozens of so-called mediums hold unauthorized Houdini séances. It has been said that if anyone could escape death and come back with a message it would be Houdini.

No message has ever come.

Bibliography

Christopher, Milbourne. *Houdini: The Untold Story*. New York: Thomas Y. Crowell Co, 1969

_____, *The Illustrated History of Magic*. New York: Thomas Y. Crowell Co, 1973

Fleischman, Sid. *Escape! The Story of The Great Houdini*. New York: Greenwillow Books, 2008

Gibson, Walter B. *The Original Houdini Scrapbook*. New York: Sterling Publishing, 1977

_____, personal written account of Houdini in Philadelphia. *Mahatmaland*. Tom Ewing, editor. 2009

Gresham, William Lindsay. *Houdini, The Man Who Walked Through Walls*. New York: Henry Holt, 1959

Henning, Doug. With Charles Reynolds. *Houdini: His Legend and His Magic*. New York: Warner Books, 1977

Houdini, Harry. *A Magician Among Spirits, The Original Manuscript*. Washington D.C.: Kaufman and Greenberg, 1996

Kalush, William and Larry Sloman. *The Secret Life of Houdini*. New York: Atria Books, 2006 I highly recommend the complete two-volume edition available at mcmagicwords.com

Kellock, Harold. *Houdini, His Life Story.* New York: Harcourt, Brace and Co., 1928

Silverman, Kenneth. *Houdini!!! The Career of Ehrich Weiss.* New York: HarperCollins, 1996

Steinmeyer, Jim. *Hiding the Elephant.* New York: Carrol & Graf, 2003 Please buy it direct from the author, jimsteinmeyer.com

Sugar, Bert Randolph and The Amazing Randi. *Presenting Houdini, His Life and Art.* New York: Grosset & Dunlap, 1976

Weltman, Manny. *Houdini: Escape into Legend, The early Years: 1862-1900.* Van Nuys, CA: Finders/Seekers Enterprises, 1993

Williams, Beryl and Samuel Epstein. *The Great Houdini.* New York: Scholastic Book Services, 14th Printing, 1971

Please support the magical arts by visiting and supporting:

The American Museum of Magic
americanmuseumofmagic.org

The Conjuring Arts Research Center
Conjuringarts.org

Books by William Pack

The Essential Houdini

The Essential P.T. Barnum

The Essential Great Chicago Fire

The Essential Edgar Allan Poe

Available through williampack.com

"If you want to watch a group of adults mesmerized at an event, invite William. Three weeks later, those who attended still comment on the program. William captivated us with his stories. He brings energy, wit, and fascinating props and illustrations to a terrific program that will stay with you and your patrons. He engages the audience at every step of the program, entertains and educates with a twinkle in his eye."
-Elke Saylor Muskego Library, WI

William is available for magic performances or educational programs customized for your event. For more information, please visit williampack.com

To contact William, email: bill@williampack.com